THE WOOLEN INDUSTRY OF THE MIDWEST

NORMAN L. CROCKETT

THE WOOLEN INDUSTRY
OF THE MIDWEST

The University Press of Kentucky

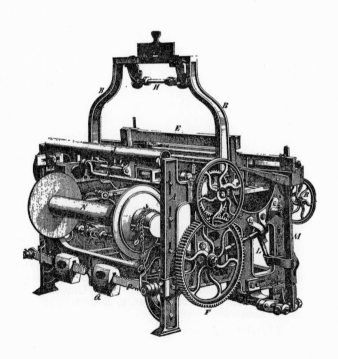

Title page illustration courtesy the Bettmann Archive, Inc.

Standard Book Number: 8131-1195-1

Library of Congress Catalog Card Number: 75-111505

Copyright © 1970 by The University Press of Kentucky

A statewide cooperative scholarly publishing agency serving Berea College, Centre College of Kentucky, Eastern Kentucky University, Kentucky State College, Morehead State University, Murray State University, University of Kentucky, University of Louisville, and Western Kentucky University.

Editorial and Sales Offices: Lexington, Kentucky 40506

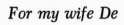
For my wife De

Contents

Preface

The contribution of small companies to America's economic development is easily forgotten in this age of business conglomerates. As late as 1954, firms employing fewer than one hundred workers constituted over 90 percent of all businesses in the United States. Such companies supplied only one-fifth of the nation's total manufacturing output, but even the most enthusiastic proponent of large-scale enterprise recognizes that without them the economy would have ceased to function. Also, historians have neglected the significant role of small manufacturing in the settlement and growth of the American West. Perhaps because of their preoccupation with the study of western agriculture and mining, and the short duration of their existence in any one region, scholars have neglected such pioneer manufacturing enterprises as barrel factories, breweries, brick yards, paper plants, rope walks, wagon works, and woolen mills.

Following the arrival of merchants along with a few custom-order artisans, businessmen entered newly developing areas to construct small manufacturing and processing plants aimed at providing frequently needed goods and services to residents within a few miles of each factory. Since the output flowing from this type of production was normally low in value relative to its bulk, residentiary manufacturers, as they are called, located businesses close to markets. High freight charges on commodities shipped into the region, coupled with a close proximity to raw products and markets, offered pioneer manufacturers important locational advantages over potential competitors outside the area. Such firms could realize a profit by providing goods suited to the particular needs of rural and small-town consumers and priced within their capacity to pay. Specialization began with residentiary manufacturing as well as factory production for delivery to final demand. Therefore, these companies constituted an intermediate step in the transition from a self-sufficient agrarian region to modern industrialization.

All areas of the United States experienced the residentiary phase of manufacturing during their formative period when population was scattered and internal transportation was primitive. Thus, for purposes of studying this type of enterprise, the selection of a specific region and the exact delineation of its geographic or political boundaries is relatively unimportant. However, as I have defined it, the states of Illinois, Indiana, Iowa, Michigan, Minnesota, Missouri, Ohio, and Wisconsin constitute the Middle West. Although woolen mills comprised only one of a number of residentiary industries which arose to serve midwesterners, there were, in 1870, 881 of them in the region. My study ranges from their organization and location in the early 1860s to their struggle for survival once the Midwest gained relatively inexpensive intra- and interregional transportation after 1900. An analysis of changes in the midwestern economy during this period has been necessary because pioneer woolen mills were primarily market-oriented and, therefore, very susceptible to any forces which affected that market.

I am grateful to Professors Lewis Atherton and Harold Woodman of the University of Missouri for their guidance. I owe a special debt to Mrs. Manfred Weber, Shawnee Mission, Kansas, for permitting me to examine her private collection of material on the Watkins Mill. To F. Harwood Orbison, president, Appleton Mills, Appleton, Wisconsin, and Robert W. Klemer, president, Faribault Woolen Mill, Faribault, Minnesota, go my special thanks for their willingness to open company records to me, for clarifying many ideas, and answering questions on the manufacture of woolen textiles. Portions of chapters three and four previously appeared in *Agricultural History* as an article on the marketing of wool in the nineteenth century, and are used here with the kind permission of the editors.

As the Harvard-Newcomen Fellow in Business and Economic History during 1967–1968, I benefited greatly from the opportunity to present and discuss my research at meetings of the Business History Group. Professors Ralph Hidy and Arthur H. Cole read portions of the manuscript and gave freely of their time, while James Baughman, Arthur M. Johnson, and Fritz Redlich constantly raised questions and suggested numerous methods for clarification and improvement. Finally, to my wife, Delores Sanders Crockett, typist, mother of four, and constructive critic of poorly written history, a mere thank you hardly seems adequate. Her continued encouragement and support throughout the preparation of this study made it not only much easier, but in large part possible.

An Earhart Fellowship in Economic and Business History from the Relm Foundation, Ann Arbor, Michigan, funds made available to me as the Harvard-Newcomen Fellow, and research grants from the University of Missouri at Rolla helped to finance this study.

THE WOOLEN INDUSTRY OF THE MIDWEST

CHAPTER I

The Eastern Background

Between the first American colonization and the Civil War the manufacture of woolen textiles along the Atlantic Coast shifted largely from home to mill, from handtools to machines, from a function of self-contained living to commercial enterprise. To bring about that transformation millions of men and women, working singly and collectively, generated a capacity to buy finished goods while, at the same time, a few others applied an accumulated knowledge about wool, men, and machines to change the methods of woolen production. In other words, the American people, through cultural borrowing and their own ingenuity, effected fundamental alterations in both supply and demand markets that characterized the woolen textile industry in 1865.

Colonial America looked to the merchants' ships of the Atlantic Community to supply manufactured goods and to transport raw materials to the world market. Despite the availability of European manfactures, many Americans were either isolated or could not afford to purchase them and quickly turned to household manufacturing. Most colonial homes produced a myriad of products, but woolen textiles comprised one of the most universal commodities of domestic production. Flocks of sheep kept by many northern farmers provided the necessary wool for spinning and weaving when inclement weather prohibited outdoor work.[1]

Whether in colonial times or later, production of woolen cloth involved eight basic functions. Raw wool was sorted, washed, dyed, carded, spun into yarn, and woven into cloth which was then fulled and finished. Aside from weaving, carding and fulling constituted the most laborious and monotonous tasks faced by household woolen manufacturers. The carder, quite often one of the family children, repeatedly combed small lots of wool between two brushes studded with wire teeth until the fleece formed a soft, extended rope, or roving, ready for the spinning wheel. Since woven cloth fresh from the loom was stiff and uneven in texture, a fulling process became necessary. Fulling required soaking the material in warm soapy water while beating it with heavy wooden mallets in order to soften the fabric and make it more pliable.[2]

Several American colonies proposed inducements to encourage both woolgrowing and manufacturing. Between 1660 and 1682, Connecticut and Massachusetts attempted to regulate cloth quality, while Virginia and Maryland extended tobacco bounties for domestically produced woolens. Maryland, Massachusetts, and Virginia levied taxes to establish spinning schools, hoping thereby to aid the poor, create skilled workers, and alleviate shortages. Through bounties and tax reductions, several colonial governments sought to promote sheep raising. Although such laws may have encouraged a few farmers to expand flocks, the poor quality of native fleece plagued the woolen industry for decades.[3]

Such legislation coupled with increasing quantities of domestic textiles produced a conflict of interests between the colonies and Great Britain. The Woolens Act of 1699 prohibited the colonists from loading woolens or raw wool on ships or carts for export, and Parliament proposed a law that, had it passed, would have prevented the sale of domestically produced woolens. Beginning in 1718, Parliament enacted a series of statutes

1. Carl Bridenbaugh, *The Colonial Craftsman* (New York, 1950), 34–35.
2. Colonial fulling parties served a similar purpose. At such gatherings people sat barefooted in a circle around large pieces of soggy cloth which were thoroughly trounced and kicked.
3. Marcus Wilson Jernegan, *The American Colonies, 1492–1750* (New York, 1959), 173; Victor S. Clark, *History of Manufactures in the United States, 1607–1860* (Washington, D.C., 1916), 34–35, 44; Frederick G. Jensen, *Capital Growth in Early America* (New York, 1965), 80.

to protect British supremacy in the woolen textile markets of the world.[4]

It is doubtful, however, if the Woolens Act and subsequent legislation had a significant impact on American output. In most areas the poor quality of homespun fabrics offered little competition to British imports. Furthermore, several Americans considered English broadcloth the ultimate in finery, and for some, garments of imported material provided a badge of social distinction for which price was not a major consideration. While imported broadcloth retailed for two to three dollars per yard, linsey-woolsey, a coarse fabric of flax and wool, sold for as little as fifteen cents. Expensive transportation between colonies, availability of domestic materials in the home and of imported goods, and the generally low level of income kept the volume of intercolonial trade in woolens at a minimum.[5] Colonial producers proved incapable of competing with the British in quality of output because they lacked the investment capital, quality wools, and skilled textile workers possessed by England. Moreover, British world trade provided a sufficiently large market to permit specialization and division of labor within the English industry. As late as 1760, after observing New England's manufacturing plants, the Reverend Andrew Burnaby noted that residents in Massachusetts "also endeavor to make woollens, [sic] but have not yet been able to bring them to any degree of perfection; indeed it is an article in which I think they will not easily succeed."[6]

The manufacture of wool represented a unique pattern of industrial development. Some industries grew from household manufacturing to custom-order production and then to the integrated factory. Of course, economic progress seldom proved to

---

4. Rolla M. Tryon, *Household Manufactures in the United States, 1640–1860* (Chicago, 1917), 25.

5. Clark, *History of Manufactures*, 108, 140–41; Mary Alice Hanna, "The Trade of the Delaware District before the Revolution," *Smith College Studies in History* 2 (1917): 259.

6. Andrew Burnaby, *Travels through the Middle Settlements in North America in the Years 1759 and 1760 with Observations upon the State of the Colonies* (Ithaca, N.Y., 1960), 97.

be so simple. Tradition, geographic isolation, and economic necessity discouraged rapid transitions. Variations frequently appeared in several sectors, and at any given time an industry might exhibit all three types of production, along with a combination or modification of them, operating concurrently. Recognition of such variables, however, fails to destroy the validity of attempting to categorize industrial growth in the past. Stages, like economic models, provide convenient reference points which aid in the reconstruction of actual developments.[7]

Family members composed the major production unit in household manufacturing. They often provided the raw material, labor, tools, and consumed all the finished product. In time, some families produced a surplus beyond their own immediate needs which they marketed in exchange for other commodities. When artisans, who possessed special skills and owned their own tools, established small shops, families frequently supplied them with raw material to be worked into a finished product on a custom basis. In payment, most artisans accepted cash, a service, another marketable commodity, or a portion of the finished material.

Given adequate local demand and a supply of capital, some handicraftsmen purchased their own raw materials and produced manufactured goods to fill direct orders from customers. The withdrawal of raw material and tools from households to artisan workshops constituted the key element which distinguished custom-order production from household manufacturing. With increased prosperity, a few artisans fabricated finished goods in advance of custom orders and such readymade items were either displayed at the shop, peddled from door to door, or hawked in the local market.

7. For a complete discussion of stages of industrial development, consult Tryon, *Household Manufactures*, 243–301, and Norman S. B. Gras, *Industrial Evolution* (Cambridge, Mass., 1930), 1–49. More recently, Herman Freudenberger and Fritz Redlich have argued for a new model of industrial stages based on a criteria of capital and control, and one which distinguishes between capital-intensive and capital-extensive industries. See "The Industrial Development of Europe: Reality, Symbols, Images," *Kyklos* no. 3, 17 (1964): 272–403.

The transformation from custom-order to factory production was sometimes a long process. In the factory, the worker received payment for his labor in wages or goods and services, and no longer owned the tools and raw materials with which he worked. Although the grouping under one roof of many artisans using handtools induced some savings, the introduction of power machinery increased output while lowering production costs. The resulting economies of scale provided the major inducement behind factory formation. However, because of the skill involved in each step of fabrication, wool manufacturing offered stubborn resistance to production changes.

In households, women and children converted raw wool into finished material, which was then sewn into family garments. An outside tailor might occasionally be employed to make clothing, or, if the family was prosperous, the services of an itinerant weaver might be utilized. In most cases, however, few artisans beyond the immediate family circle handled the actual fabrication of cloth.

The expanding production of woolen fabrics in American homes, plus the demand for carded wool by the increased number of household spinners, made fulling and carding feasible commercial operations. Inventors had successfully applied waterpower to both fulling mills and carding machines by 1795, and within fifteen years carders and fullers outside the home probably carded more wool and dressed more cloth than did household manufacturers. Unlike typical artisans, commercial fullers and carders failed to produce a finished commodity; their services simply involved two steps in production which substantially reduced the labor and time of family members. Thus, the development of power machinery for carding and fulling, temporarily strengthened the economic position of household wool manufacturing.[8]

Private attempts before 1800 at concentrating all stages of woolen cloth production under one roof proved abortive. Since spinning and weaving required one worker per spinning frame

8. Curtis P. Nettels, *The Emergence of a National Economy, 1775–1815* (New York, 1962), 276.

or loom, little was gained by housing all laborers in one plant. A reduction of transfer costs in moving materials from one artisan to another usually resulted, but normal factory economies of scale were unattainable. Moreover, the poor character of native wool, coupled with the varying skills of handloom and spinning wheel operatives, prevented the perfection of a product of consistent high quality. To utilize best the talents of local artisans, a few entrepreneurs employed the cottage or putting-out system, in which some steps of production were delegated to laborers who resided in their own homes or small workshops and processed the raw materials of the manufacturer.[9] Therefore, most early American woolen "factories" represented nothing more than a fulling mill and carding machine flanked by the houses and shops of local spinners and weavers.

Spinning and weaving constituted the major bottlenecks in early American factory production of woolens for many years. In developing nations the demand for cheap textiles is highly price elastic, and some manufacturers recognized that the introduction of power machinery to reduce input costs and expand output could increase both consumption and profits. Therefore, a number of Americans showed interest in the spinning machines and power looms developed in the British cotton and woolen industries. England, of course, had enacted laws prohibiting the export of textile appliances, knowledge, or skilled labor, but such statutes failed to deter some manufacturers from borrowing what they could not buy or build.

The methods employed by Thomas Attewood Digges typified the efforts of several Americans who attempted to coax English and Irish textile workers to the United States. No doubt perceiving the nearly unlimited market for textiles, Digges first concentrated on transporting both skilled laborers and up-to-date machinery. Smuggling bulky machines, however, proved to be a formidable task, so Digges then sought to entice artisans who

9. Peter Stewart, "A Brief History of the Peace Dale Manufacturing Company, 1802–1918," *Textile History Review* 4 (January 1963): 12–14; U.S. Bureau of Statistics, *Wool and Manufactures of Wool* (Washington, D.C., 1888), xlvii.

could build such equipment or tried to obtain drawings of these machines. William Pearce, who emigrated at Digges's invitation, suffered the fate of several other English migrants in that he failed to secure patents for his textile "inventions."[10]

Men like Digges brought some trained workers and a few machines to America, but on the eve of the Revolution wool manufacturing remained in a modified artisan stage of development. Handicraftsmen operated tiny carding, fulling, and weaving shops, worked the material of others, and customarily accepted payment in farm products or in the commodity which they processed. Manufacturers attempting to organize factories faced capital shortages, which lowered their ability to offer competitive wages and necessitated the operation of old, and often inadequate machinery. The millowners' lack of knowledge concerning very elementary processes and the poor quality of native fleece made competition with foreign imports difficult. Thus, in the domestic market, American woolen mills could not compete with British textiles, and household manufacturers supplied the bulk of the demand for coarse-quality cloth.

During the Revolutionary War the rapid expansion of household production of woolens was fostered by patriotism and necessity. A few government dignitaries took public pride in their homespun suits, but politics and a shortage of foreign fabrics made such action palatable when imports ceased. Most people clothed themselves adequately, and a few families even managed to produce a surplus for market. After the Treaty of Paris, however, Americans again looked to English manufacturers to supply fine-quality woolens, and per capita consumption of British textiles continued to increase from 1783 to the turn of the century.[11]

10. Carroll W. Pursell, Jr., "Thomas Digges and William Pearce: An Example of the Transit of Technology," *William and Mary Quarterly* 21 (October 1964): 551–60.

11. In 1790 British woolen imports into the United States amounted to approximately £1,500,000, which represented 30 percent of Britain's total woolen export, and nine years later such imports had reached 40 percent. Herbert Heaton, "Benjamin Gott and the Anglo-American Cloth Trade," *Journal of Economic and Business History* 2 (November 1929): 147.

A substantial portion of the funds which financed factory construction prior to and during the War of 1812 came from mercantile profits, but the shift from commerce to manufacturing was relatively slow. Merchants were reluctant to withdraw capital from trade to invest in factories, and many carried on mercantile activities long after they made manufacturing investments. Perhaps because they were familiar with the product, textile merchants who imported and sold woolens seemed most inclined to invest in woolen factories. However, many refused to loan funds for carding and fulling mills, since they wanted a product to enhance their trading operations. The profits of some manufacturers encouraged others to enter the race—the closed outlet for raw materials plus the increased ratio of the price of finished goods to input costs, lured capital into manufacturing with an expectation of large returns.[12]

Some capital for woolen mills emanated from the profits of other manufacturing enterprises: William Young and Joshua and Vincent Gilpin of Delaware built textile mills from papermaking profits; Robert Phillips, owner of a factory on the Brandywine, had operated a gristmill before 1812; and the woolen plant of E. I. DuPont and Peter Barduy grew from capital accumulated in gunpowder manufacturing. Partnerships offered mutual advantages in alleviating shortages of money and skills. For example, throughout the War of 1812, John Phillips produced woolen thread at his Delaware mill. John Butler, a fuller, and Charles Briggs, a finisher, later joined Phillips in a partnership which pooled machinery, funds, and expertise.[13]

Despite previous injections of capital, the American woolen industry exhibited signs of instability in 1815. In the domestic

12. Samuel Eliot Morison, *The Maritime History of Massachusetts, 1783–1860* (Boston, 1921), 215; Margaret E. Martin, "Merchants and Trade of the Connecticut River Valley, 1750–1820," *Smith College Studies in History* 24 (1938): 184; Nettels, *Emergence of a National Economy,* 338.

13. George H. Gibson, "The Growth of the Woolen Industry in Nineteenth Century Delaware," *Textile History Review* 5 (October 1964): 125, 129.

10

market, wartime scarcity had created an artificial demand and few factories could withstand English competition once trade was resumed. Mills held large cloth inventories, consumers complained of inferior material, and some factories owned excessive quantities of raw wool purchased at inflated prices.[14] In addition, household manufacturers still enjoyed their entrenched position in the market. Homespun experienced a slow death, and not until eastern farmers faced western grain and livestock competition after the 1820s, did household manufacturing show indications of decline. Only then did farmers in the East realize that they must specialize in serving local urban markets with perishable foodstuffs that could not be shipped from the West. Given such an unstable situation, many woolen mills simply closed their doors when the first great postwar wave of British textiles hit the American market in late 1815.

Like the American Revolution, the War of 1812 failed to provide economic liberation from English and European manufacturers. However, the period between 1790 and 1816 witnessed slow but significant changes in the American economy. Embargo, nonintercourse, and war altered foreign trade patterns while the subsidiary sectors of banking, brokerage, and insurance blossomed to serve the reexport and carrying trades. In turn, shipping and reexport fostered urban growth and stimulated local manufacturing to supply the new internal market. And the psychological impact of a new and stronger central government encouraged increased investments by entrepreneurs.[15]

Not surprisingly in an undeveloped economy, woolen manufacturers won support for their plea for direct aid from legislators and the colonial practice of subsidizing manufacturing continued throughout the antebellum years. States provided loans, offered tax exemptions, and granted lottery privileges. As only one of numerous examples, Massachusetts gave one firm

14. Clark, *History of Manufactures,* 379.
15. Douglass C. North, *The Economic Growth of the United States, 1790–1860* (Englewood Cliffs, N.J., 1961), 49–51.

the right to label its product with the state seal, thus backing the commodity with the prestige of the commonwealth.[16] Therefore, government aid to woolen factories was common practice when millowners urged Congress to impose a protective tariff on imported textiles in 1815. In response, Congress enacted major tariffs on woolens in 1816 and 1824, and a few states offered distressed woolen factories special tax privileges.

When state relief and federal tariff alike failed to halt the flood of British woolens, beleaguered manufacturers asked for and received additional protection. The tariff of 1828 contained a provision for a minimum duty on imports which American manufacturers argued would eliminate undervaluation of imported woolens by dishonest customs officials.[17] Regardless of the claims and charges of tariff supporters and detractors, the effect of the 1828 tariff is debatable, since by that time most American woolen mills were well established, if not overly prosperous, and no longer needed the protection afforded infant industries in a developing nation. Henry C. Carey and others continued to demand protection for American manufacturing, but the chatter of tariff argumentation subsided rapidly after 1833, perhaps as a result of the good times ushered in with the increase of American agricultural exports and the lowering of English tariff rates in the 1840s.

American woolen manufacturers began a gradual conversion from hand to power machinery in the 1820s, and by the 1840s the transition had accelerated. However, American inventiveness seemed lacking in the field of woolen machine technology and most of the inventions between 1840 and the Civil War consisted of minor modifications and improvements of existing

16. Oscar and Mary F. Handlin, *Commonwealth: A Study of the Role of Government in the American Economy: Massachusetts, 1774–1861* (New York, 1947), 111–12; Joseph S. Davis, *Essays in the Earlier History of American Corporations,* 2 vols. (Cambridge, Mass., 1917) 2: 266–68.

17. Chester W. Wright, *Wool-Growing and the Tariff* (Cambridge, Mass., 1910), 41, 68; Frank W. Taussig, *The Tariff History of the United States* (New York, 1923), 37–45.

machines.[18] Large capital requirements and a shallow internal market foiled several early attempts at establishment of separate firms for the manufacture of textile appliances, but after 1845 machinists accomplished a complete withdrawal of machine shops from factories. Thereafter, American woolen mills no longer had to depend upon their own ingenuity or foreign producers to supply them with original equipment or replacement parts.[19]

The employment of women and children in American woolen mills increased with the introduction of power machinery. Heavy strain on the vertical, or warp threads, had previously prevented woolen factories from adopting power looms, and as a consequence of the strength necessary to operate the hand-loom, men normally constituted well over one-half of the labor force in early mills. With the application of power to nearly all steps in production, however, millowners hired entire families since women and children could then be used effectively. Unskilled labor became easier to find, but despite the importation of foreign operatives and the introduction of programs to train workers, prior to the Civil War most American woolen mills faced periodic shortages of skilled laborers.[20]

Auctions had been a familiar sight in the pre-Revolutionary era, and such sales remained an important feature of American marketing in the decade after 1815. Since American shop-

18. The Goulding Condenser in 1826, which automatically passed the roving from one carding machine to another, and a self-cleaning card in 1853, constituted the only major American contributions to woolen machine technology before the Civil War.

19. W. Paul Strassmann, *Risk and Technological Innovation: American Manufacturing Methods during the Nineteenth Century* (Ithaca, N.Y., 1959), 70–77. For detailed studies of two early textile machine builders, see Thomas R. Navin, *The Whitin Machine Works since 1831* (Cambridge, Mass., 1950), and George S. Gibb, *The Saco-Lowell Shops* (Cambridge, Mass., 1950).

20. Norman Ware, *The Industrial Worker, 1840–1860* (Gloucester, Mass., 1959), 61–64; William A. Sullivan, "The Industrial Revolution and the Factory Operative in Pennsylvania," *Pennsylvania Magazine of History and Biography* 78 (October 1954): 485–87; Gibson, "Delaware Woolen Industry," 145–48.

keepers and merchants could not normally meet auction prices, they agitated to restrict the method. However, state prohibition and mild tax restrictions proved incapable of preventing the fake labeling and other deceptive practices of some auctioneers. Despite their public denunciations, many merchants joined their competitors by selling through auctions. This in turn only compounded the problem by delaying the rapid development of an efficient internal marketing structure. Although auctions were no more unique to woolens than other commodities, this method of wholesaling and retailing found wide adoption by woolen importers.[21] Between 1822 and 1830, for example, 70 percent of the dry goods marketed in New York are said to have been sold at auction.[22]

The close of the 1830s saw the relative demise of the auction system, as foreign textile manufacturers tended to concentrate on filling large, direct orders from American merchants rather than selling through a host of small importers and agents. American commission houses assumed increasing importance in the wholesale distribution of textiles, and such firms accepted goods from eastern manufacturers, deducting charges for transportation, storage, insurance, and a selling commission. In addition, commission merchants collected and received funds, advanced short term loans, and advised mills on the correct types and quantities of fabrics to produce. After 1840, several commission houses concentrated on special lines, such as dress goods or suiting, and became the exclusive sales agents for a few large factories. Since these companies were closely tied to the mills they served, most suffered when depressions hit the woolen industry.[23]

21. Fred Mitchell Jones, *Middlemen in the Domestic Trade of the United States* (Urbana, Ill., 1937), 35–43; Lewis E. Atherton, "Auctions as a Threat to American Business in the Eighteen Twenties and Thirties," *Bulletin of the Business Historical Society* 11 (November 1937): 104–107.
22. Norman S. B. Gras and Henrietta M. Larson, *Casebook in American Business History* (New York, 1939), 678.
23. Arthur Harrison Cole, *The American Wool Manufacture* (Cambridge, Mass., 1926) 1: 208–15.

In the late antebellum period eastern consumers displayed a tendency toward increased fashion in dress and demanded a lightweight woolen cloth that could be easily fabricated into attractive clothing. And, by 1865 worsted material, a relative newcomer to the American woolen industry, offered strong competition to woolen manufacturers. Worsteds, which used long, coarse wool and required more elaborate machinery than woolens, were scarce in America prior to 1840. The lack of a native wool suitable for worsted manufacturing was alleviated with establishment of Canadian reciprocity in 1854, and in that same year America's first combing machines commenced operation. By comparison to woolen mills, worsted factories were giants. In 1860, for example, the bulk of American worsted cloth came from three firms which had an average capital investment of over one million dollars.[24]

The Civil War's long-range effect on American industrial growth is debatable, but for a while, woolen manufacturers basked in prosperity. At first, northern mills could not meet Union army demand, but woolen producers assured the government that needs would be filled quickly. Although new factories opened, cotton mills converted to wool, and plant operating time increased, the Union was forced to buy cloth worth approximately $800,000 from England, much to the consternation and embarrassment of American millowners.[25] To silence the resulting storm of criticism, the army quartermaster finally agreed to cease all foreign purchases and to accept domestic material of varied colors. As a result, a few gray-clad soldiers from the North were shot and killed by their own comrades.[26]

24. Manchester Print Works, Manchester, New Hampshire; Pacific Mills, Lawrence, Massachusetts; and the Hamilton Woolen Works, Southbridge, Massachusetts.

25. Emerson D. Fite, *Social and Industrial Conditions in the North during the Civil War* (New York, 1910), 83; Victor S. Clark, "Manufacturing Development during the Civil War," in *The Economic Impact of the American Civil War,* ed. Ralph Andreano (Cambridge, Mass., 1962), 46.

26. Fred A. Shannon, *The Organization and Administration of the Union Army, 1861–1865,* 2 vols. (Cleveland, Ohio, 1928) 1: 84, 90–93; Bell I. Wiley, *The Life of Billy Yank* (New York, 1952), 22.

To meet the heavy demand for their product, American sheep producers expanded flocks during the war, thus creating at its close a raw wool surplus matched only by the increased inventory of finished cloth. Wool and woolens markets were thoroughly glutted by 1865, and in that year the wholesale price index of textiles reached its peak and then began a steady descent which lasted through 1870. Within two years after Appomattox many farmers slaughtered sheep for their mutton and hides as wool prices also tumbled. Although woolgrowers as a group publicly opposed the tariff in theory, declining profits after 1865 prompted them to praise the merits of a high protective barrier against foreign wool.[27]

Manufacturers, on the other hand, also sought additional tariff protection, and the possibility of open political conflict between sheep farmers and woolen producers increased substantially in 1865 with the formation of both the National Association of Wool Manufacturers and the National Wool Growers Association. The two groups, however, soon recognized that cooperation provided the best solution to their problems and the end result was united support for the Wool and Woolens Act of 1867. The new law retained the compensation system included in the Morrill Tariff of 1861, which combined protection for woolgrowers and wool manufacturers. Imported woolens paid an ad valorem duty, plus an additional charge per pound, designed to compensate the manufacturer for a duty on imported raw wool.[28]

General agreement between sheep farmers and millowners lasted much longer than the harmony within the National Association of Wool Manufacturers. Representatives from the carpet and worsted sections appear to have wielded the most power inside the new association, and woolen producers complained that they paid a higher import duty on raw material

27. Robert P. Sharkey, *Money, Class, and Party: An Economic Study of Civil War and Reconstruction* (Baltimore, Md., 1959), 147; Howard K. Beale, "The Tariff and Reconstruction," *American Historical Review* 35 (January 1930): 283–85.
28. Taussig, *Tariff History*, 195–218.

than did worsted manufacturers.[29] Since American consumers were exhibiting an increasing propensity to buy worsted rather than woolen fabrics, several wool manufacturers withdrew from the organization and later formed a separate trade association to handle their own lobbying.[30]

In the three decades before the Civil War, the American woolen industry manifested a general trend of growth and consolidation. While the number of woolen factories declined by over five hundred in the 1850s, total capital investment in woolen mills increased by over 18 percent, an indication of the enhanced utilization of machinery. By 1865, all sections of the country contained woolen mills, but New England claimed the largest plants and the greatest number of firms. Increased capitalization ousted many small producers. Large factories sometimes ran at losses to reduce average costs, prices declined, and smaller and less efficient firms found competition difficult.

High ratios of capital to labor, however, indicated that by the close of the Civil War the American wool manufacture had advanced well beyond the struggling steps of its infancy and had finally reached maturity. The availability of modern machines, skilled labor, and pools of investment capital had encouraged many businessmen to manufacture woolen textiles in an effort to supply the increasing domestic market of the United States. Yet, while these changes were in progress, the market for woolen fabrics was constantly expanding as people moved to newly developing regions. Some eastern manufacturers sought to produce cloth and yarn for shipment to the new market, while a few entrepreneurs perceived the possibilities of constructing woolen factories in the West.

29. Erastus Bigelow from the carpet industry, and J. Wiley Edwards of Pacific Mills, a worsted producer, were considered the major spokesmen for these two interests. In 1869, for example, Bigelow was president of the association and served on the Executive Committee, while Edwards sat on both the Finance and Executive committees.

30. Stanley Coben, "Northeastern Business and Radical Reconstruction," *Mississippi Valley Historical Review* 46 (June 1959): 74–75; Harry James Brown, "The Fleece and the Loom: Wool Growers and Wool Manufacturers during the Civil War," *Business History Review* 29 (March 1955): 18.

CHAPTER II

Wool Manufacturers
Enter the Middle West

Historians continue to debate numerous aspects of American economic development, but few deny the rapidity of settlement in the West. While many eastern towns suffered heavy population losses after 1830, several once-isolated western villages blossomed into major cities in less than twenty years. Chicago's population, for example, doubled twice in the ten years after 1847 and by the late fifties the city was already destined to become the center of midwestern transportation. The agents of cities, counties, states, and railroads bombarded the Atlantic Coast and Europe with promotional literature aimed at potential immigrants, and each assured the prospective settler that his immediate locality would soon be the commercial and financial hub of the West.[1] Although poor organization and overenthusiasm limited many state and local immigration programs, on the eve of the Civil War, Ohio, Illinois, Indiana, and Missouri ranked third, fourth, sixth, and eighth in population respectively, and the eight states of the Middle West contained nearly nine million inhabitants.[2]

Prior to 1830, most midwestern farmers remained isolated from the national economy, and except for those settlers living near water routes, a commercial market for agricultural produce was either nonexistent or confined primarily to the immediate neighborhood. Only furs, livestock, and a few other commodities could withstand overland shipment to the seaboard. Adlard Welby clearly perceived the problem of inadequate and expensive transportation in the West after his visit to George Flower's English Prairie in Illinois. Writing around 1820, Welby recognized that the local population failed to constitute a market of sufficient depth to consume the output of the area, and that these farmers must resign themselves to "laying the foundation of future fortune for their posterity."[3]

While Welby wrote, however, significant changes were already underway. Perfection of the cotton gin and the growing demand of the English textile industry for raw material prompted the rapid adoption of the plantation system in the rich soils of the Deep South. With increased specialization on cotton culture in the South, middlewestern small farmers soon found a ready market for their agricultural commodities.[4] Receipts of interior produce at New Orleans amounted to over $22,000,000 in 1830, and the total value doubled in each of the next three decades.[5] Armed with the income from the sale of their products, midwestern farmers increased demands for northeastern and European manufactures.

Eastern merchants and commission houses were cognizant of the growing market for manufactured goods in the West. New York's astounding success with the Erie Canal after 1825 initi-

1. For a discussion of the immigration programs of several midwestern states, see Norman L. Crockett, "A Study of Confusion: Missouri's Immigration Program, 1865–1916," *Missouri Historical Review* 57 (April 1963): 248–60; Theodore C. Blegen, "The Competition of the Northwestern States for Immigrants," *Wisconsin Magazine of History* 3 (September 1919): 3–29; Maurice D. Baxter, "Encouragement of Immigration to the Middle West during the Era of the Civil War," *Indiana Magazine of History* 46 (March 1950): 25–38.

2. U.S. Department of Commerce, Bureau of the Census, Ninth Census, *The Statistics of the Population of the United States, 1870* (Washington, D.C., 1872), 1: 3.

3. Adlard Welby, *A Visit to North America and the English Settlements in Illinois* (London, 1821) in *Early Western Travels*, ed. Reuben Gold Thwaites, 32 vols. (Cleveland, Ohio, 1906), 12: 257–58.

4. Guy Stevens Callender, *Selections from the Economic History of the United States, 1765–1860* (Boston, 1909), 272–73; Louis Bernard Schmidt, "Internal Commerce and the Development of a National Economy before 1860," *Journal of Political Economy* 47 (December 1939): 803–806.

5. Emory R. Johnson and others, *History of Domestic and Foreign Commerce of the United States*, 2 vols. (Washington, D.C., 1915), 1: 243.

ated a wave of canal building. New Jersey, New York, Ohio, and Pennsylvania, equipped with foreign capital from the sale of state bonds, chartered banks and corporations, giving direct aid to canal construction. Hardly had the canal mania reached its zenith than railroads began laying track, first to fill the gaps in water transport, and later to tap more of the hinterland. This activity increased city land values and encouraged even greater investments.[6] By the mid-1840s, the volume of western grain going over the lake route exceeded that being floated down river to New Orleans.[7]

Despite liberal state support, midwestern transportation facilities failed to keep pace with the region's growing population. Although western farm staples and eastern manufactured goods were exchanged, the United States lacked a completely national marketing system until well after the Civil War. Frozen streams and low water, differentials in railroad track gauge, inadequate feeder lines, high freight rates, and the steady advance of population limited the easy exchange of products.[8] On cargoes bound for villages not immediately adjacent to a canal, railroad, or river, transport costs exhibited few signs of reduction; town-to-town or farm-to-market road improvement did not constitute an important characteristic of the "transportation revolution." Even those communities on navigable rivers often found consistent freight service a slow development. For example, the residents of Franklin, on the Missouri River, witnessed the dockage of a steamboat in 1826, but they waited nearly four years for regular freight and passenger service.[9]

During the early years of settlement, boats loaded with man-

6. Carter Goodrich and others, *Canals and American Economic Development* (New York, 1961), 249–55; Guy Stevens Callender, "The Early Transportation and Banking Enterprises of the States in Relation to the Growth of Corporations," *Quarterly Journal of Economics* 17 (November 1902): 159–61.

7. Harvey S. Perloff and others, *Regions, Resources, and Economic Growth* (Baltimore, Md., 1960), 115.

8. George Rogers Taylor and Irene D. Neu, *The American Railroad Network, 1861–1890* (Cambridge, Mass., 1956), 35–41.

9. Jonas Viles, "Old Franklin: A Frontier Town of the Twenties," *Mississippi Valley Historical Review* 9 (March 1923): 275.

ufactured items traveled the western rivers, distributing their wares to traders along the shore, and as early as 1810 merchants began to transport staple groceries and dry goods to small stores along the Mississippi, Missouri, and Ohio. As settlers increased in numbers and moved inland away from the rivers, merchants trekked into the interior, selected a suitable location, and began operations. The arrival of merchants in an isolated area invoked enthusiasm among residents, since most realized the economic importance of a local store. When John Beauchamp Jones established his store at Pike Bluff, Missouri, in the 1840s, "the people for miles around came in every day to inquire when the goods would arrive. . . . The beginning of a new town . . . by means of the establishment of a store there, made considerable noise in that community."[10]

A small town usually formed around the nucleus of a store, and artisans joined the new community to offer their services to area residents. A scarcity of trained labor often prompted interested citizens to contact people in the East who possessed special skills to encourage them to migrate westward. John Bergen, for example, who in 1828 moved from New Jersey to Springfield, Illinois, wrote friends in Philadelphia inviting carpenters, blacksmiths, jewelers, saddlers, shoemakers, and tailors to join him in Sangamon County.[11] Rural communities with artisan workshops usually sprang up at distances of six to twelve miles apart, so midwestern farmers had a market within one day's journey of their homes. Therefore, farmers tended increasingly to specialize in staple crops and to purchase items from rural stores which were previously manufactured by the family.[12]

Regardless of size, most frontier towns provided a great vari-

10. Luke Shortfield, *The Western Merchant* (Philadelphia, 1849), 42.

11. J. Van Fenstermaker, "A Description of Sangamon County, Illinois, in 1830," *Agricultural History* 39 (July 1965): 139.

12. Lewis E. Atherton, *Main Street on the Middle Border* (Bloomington, Ind., 1954), 3; Eugene Smolensky and Donald Ratajcak, "The Conception of Cities," *Explorations in Entrepreneurial History,* vol. 2, 2d ser. (Winter 1965): 101.

ety of goods and services to the residents of their own immediate trade area. For example, Franklin, Missouri, not only contained the usual assortment of pioneer artisans and stores in 1819, but also provided a livelihood for doctors, dentists, and lawyers. The twenty-five families who made up one town in Delaware County, Indiana, in 1850, received service from three general stores, a grocer, an inn, a shoemaker, a blacksmith, two tanners, two cabinetmakers, a miller, three carpenters, two coopers, two wagonmakers, two doctors, and a cobbler.[13]

As the density of the midwestern market increased and as per capita incomes grew, settlers in the region consumed larger quantities of manufactured goods and also demanded products of higher quality. On his tour of the western states in 1818, Estwick Evans expressed amazement at the high prices received for the large volume of eastern manufactured items shipped to Detroit.[14] And, as early as 1815, Christian Wilt's invoices of eastern merchandise for his St. Louis store illustrated the desire of local residents for finer quality clothing corresponding more closely to the styles and fashions of cities in the East. Mercantile establishments throughout the Middle West, therefore, publicized the eastern origin of their firms' inventory since such notations impressed customers.[15]

Prior to the advent of through rail service, heavy eastern goods were shipped by boat down the Ohio, or by coastal vessel to New Orleans and then upstream to interior destinations, while lighter commodities normally went overland, utilizing water routes where practicable. Transportation costs were high.

---

13. Harvey L. Carter, "Rural Indiana in Transition, 1850–1860," *Agricultural History* 20 (April 1946): 111; Viles, "Old Franklin," 274–78.

14. Estwick Evans, *A Predestrious Tour of Four Thousand Miles, through the Western States and Territories during the Winter of 1818* (Concord, Mass., 1819) in *Early Western Travels*, ed. Reuben Gold Thwaites, 32 vols. (Cleveland, Ohio, 1906), 8: 219–20.

15. Sister Marietta Jennings, *A Pioneer Merchant of St. Louis 1810–1820: The Business Career of Christian Wilt* (New York, 1939), 187; Lewis E. Atherton, *The Pioneer Merchant in Mid-America*, University of Missouri Studies, no. 2, (Columbia, Mo., 1939) 14: 116, 125.

James and Robert Aull, who operated stores in several Missouri towns in the 1830s, calculated freight charges at approximately one-fourth of the value of delivered merchandise.[16] After 1830, to supplement the annual visit of western merchants and to increase sales, eastern manufacturers dispatched drummers to the West. Such agents collected accounts, checked credit references, and filled direct orders from retailers.[17]

High overland transfer costs and irregular service encouraged a multitude of handicraftsmen and manufacturers to enter the Middle West to offer their goods and services to local residents. Artisans established small shops to finish the semi-manufactured items of household producers, or to fill direct orders from their own raw material inventories on a custom basis. The cabinetmaker, shoemaker, and tailor, therefore, became as much a part of the westward movement as the farmer, merchant, and trapper. In addition, the existence of a market lacking inexpensive inter- and intraregional transportation facilities, encouraged businessmen to construct factories which could utilize an abundant local resource and sell manufactured goods to the residents of surrounding farms and small towns. Since their raw material and market existed in the immediate locality of the firm, these residentiary industries were both market-oriented and resource-oriented.

The high cost of transportation, which in part retarded the complete development of a national market, actually protected residentiary manufacturers from larger eastern competitors. Therefore, middlewestern producers operated behind the protective barrier of high freight rates on eastern goods shipped into the region. As long as local manufacturers concentrated on low- and medium-quality products, for which there was a nearly universal demand, most could show a profit. Because such goods were low in value relative to their bulk, producers in the

16. Lewis E. Atherton, "James and Robert Aull—A Frontier Missouri Mercantile Firm," *Missouri Historical Review* 30 (October 1935): 9.
17. Theodore F. Marburg, "Manufacturer's Drummer, 1852, with Comments on Western and Southern Markets," *Bulletin of the Business Historical Society* 22 (April 1948): 108–109, 113–14.

East found that on many items profit margins were too small and sale prices too low to add high transport charges and still compete with manufacturers in the Middle West. On some items, eastern producers could undersell pioneer manufacturers in the midwestern market. However, since transportation costs as a percentage of sales were highest on low-value goods, eastern factory owners could maximize profits by producing high-value items for sale in the Middle West. Any economies of scale enjoyed by manufacturers in the East because of mass production or greater efficiency were presumably less than the transport costs to the Middle West.

In a short time, a midwestern community of any size possessed its own brewery, woolen mill, wagon factory, and paper-plant. For example, Knox County, Indiana, in 1820, contained factories which produced barrels, candles, fur hats, furniture, plows, saddles, thread, wagons, and woolen yarn.[18] Although the town of Oshkosh, Wisconsin, had a population of only 2,500 in 1853, it harbored plants which supplied area residents with barrels, beer, candles, shingles and sashes, threshing machines, wagons, and water pumps.[19] Except for minor variations, manufacturing development exhibited a similar pattern of growth in each developing region. A close examination of the factories of New England in the late colonial period, Ohio in the 1820s, and Iowa on the eve of the Civil War, show striking similarities as to type, mode of operation, and extent. Thus, the residentiary stage of manufacturing accompanied each westward surge of population.

As isolated areas of the Middle West filled with settlers, the eastern woolen industry repeated its development of previous decades with only a few minor modifications. Midwestern pioneer women, like their ancestors of the colonial period, found it necessary to take up the spinning wheel and handloom in order to provide their families with adequate clothing. Long

18. U.S. Department of Commerce, Fourth Census, 1820, *Manufactures, State of Indiana*, 205, microfilm in the Indiana State Library, Archives Division, Indianapolis.

19. John W. Hunt, *Wisconsin Gazetteer* (Madison, Wis., 1853), 167.

after local storekeepers offered imported dry goods some households continued to manufacture textiles. In writing to a friend
in 1859, one Indiana housewife claimed that in six months she
had spun thirty-five pounds of wool into yarn, had woven forty
yards of cloth, and had fashioned sixty yards of material into
family garments.[20] The extent of domestic wool manufacturing
prior to the Civil War was apparent to several people in the
Middle West. Theodore Denney, for example, an Indiana
farmer, in an 1841 letter to his brother in New England, urged
his relatives to ship him a large quantity of handcards to
Indianapolis, since the state comprised a market for "more
cards than they could produce."[21]

Hardly was the farmer established in an area before fullers
and carders set up machinery on small streams to offer their
services to local citizens. Typical of what Rolla Tryon labeled
the "mill stage," these early carding and fulling appliances
represented a small capital investment and ran only when local
demand warranted operation. For example, in 1820, one rural
Indiana carding and fulling mill, valued at six hundred dollars,
employed but one worker who ran the machinery periodically.[22]

Farmers hauled their wool to carders and fullers for processing, and in turn offered various methods of payment for the
service. The account book of William Murray, who operated a
small mill in Wayne County, Indiana, from 1847 to 1854, is
typical of such establishments which relied on the local economy for their income. In addition to cash, promissory notes, and
raw wool, Murray accepted the following in payment for carding wool and finishing cloth: bricks, credit at a local store, soap,
wheat and corn, pumpkins, apples and cider, grass seed, lum-
ber, the services of a dentist and blacksmith, and hours of labor
spent at butchering, hauling hay, and work in the mill.[23]

20. Carter, "Rural Indiana in Transition," 113–14.
21. Theodore Denney to Christopher Denney, Indianapolis, February 6, 1841, Theodore Denny Papers, in the Indiana Historical Society, Indianapolis.
22. Fourth Census, *Indiana*, 1820, 204.
23. Account Book, William Murray Woolen Mill, Wayne County,
Indiana, 1847–1853, 99–136, William Murray Woolen Mill Account
Books, in the Indiana Historical Society, Indianapolis.

25

Because of the need to utilize available water supplies, mills of all types tended to concentrate on small streams. Eli Creek, near Indianapolis contained three sawmills, a flour-and-grist mill, two carding engines, and a fulling mill around 1820.[24] Moreover, since one water wheel or small steam engine could provide motive power for several different types of machinery, one building might perhaps house equipment to grind wheat, full woolen cloth, and saw wood. For example, William Elliot's mill at St. Catherine, Missouri, in 1860, contained two carding machines, a flour mill, and distilling apparatus.[25]

With each advance of population, commercial carders moved westward. Before 1825 carding machines had crossed the Mississippi River,[26] and twenty years later Illinois, Indiana, Michigan, Ohio, and Wisconsin could each claim several Goulding Condensers, the most up-to-date machines available.[27] By 1860, carding engines could be found in every state of the Middle West, and the federal census of that year enumerated 247 in the region, with Missouri's 86 machines leading all middlewestern states.[28] Long after the establishment of full-scale woolen factories, many housewives continued to weave their own cloth, and up to the turn of the century midwestern woolen plants emphasized their custom-carding services in order to meet the demands of household manufacturers.

The putting-out or cottage system, which had represented a transitional step from custom-order to factory production in the

24. File on "Early Mill, or Mill Sites, Built Prior to 1870," in the Indiana Historical Society, Indianapolis.

25. *The History of Linn County, Missouri* (Kansas City, 1882), 676.

26. *Missouri Intelligencer*, April 22, 1823; *Jackson* (Mo.) *Independent Patriot*, May 26, 1821.

27. Proprietor of the Condensing Cards, *Statistics of the Woolen Manufactories in the United States* (New York, 1846), passim.

28. U.S. Department of Commerce, Census Office, *Manufactures of the United States in 1860: Compiled from the Original Returns of the Eighth Census* (Washington, D.C., 1865), 113, 145, 163, 276, 284, 318, 488, 658. The typical carding machine in the Middle West in 1860 represented a capital investment of less than $1,800 and, on the average, the owners normally employed less than two workers per year.

evolution of the eastern woolen industry, found virtually no counterpart in midwestern development. High population density and lack of power machinery had provided the incentive to employ eastern cottagers. In the Middle West, however, labor proved expensive because of its scarcity, and by the time the region was being settled the basic machines which had replaced hand operations had already been invented. Hence, the Midwest experienced no cottage phase of production. Fully equipped factories, which handled all steps in cloth manufacture, from sorting to finishing, sprang up in many localities where once only carding engines and fulling mills had previously operated.

Many factors influence the locational pattern of economic activity. Manufacturers locate firms in order to benefit from capital resources, raw products, labor supplies, or nearness to markets. Theoretically, the farsighted entrepreneur chooses the one location which permits the best combination of these elements, but, realistically, imperfect knowledge prohibits the selection of the perfect factory site. Chance frequently plays an important role, and quite by accident a producer may select the correct location and thus gain the upper hand over competitive firms, or, as the economy changes, all advantages may disappear.[29]

Industries in which the finished product is low in value and yet universally demanded, and in which raw materials are locally abundant, tend to disperse over a wide geographic area, with each plant attempting to serve a small market. Wool manufacturing constituted just such an industry, and businessmen established factories any place in the Middle West where local markets appeared adequate to support such enterprises. The Midwest's increases in sheep and in human population after 1850 provided a relatively good market, laborers, and sufficient quantities of raw wool, while the steam engine freed manufacturers from dependence upon streams to provide power for machinery.

29. Charles M. Tiebout, "Location Theory, Empirical Evidence, and Economic Evolution," Regional Science Association, *Papers and Proceedings* 3 (1957): 74–86.

Many early woolen mills sprang up in rather isolated areas, several miles from canals, railroads, and rivers. As examples, the Watkins Mill, first opened in 1861 in northwest Missouri, stood approximately six miles from the nearest town, and Andrew Yount built his Montgomery County, Indiana, factory four miles from Crawfordsville. In general, midwestern woolen producers constructed mills in rural areas, in or near small towns, where population density within a fifty-mile radius of the plant provided a sufficient market to consume factory output. However, with few exceptions, manufacturers avoided locating in larger cities and also tended to establish mills in areas not served by other woolen factories.[30]

Personal background information on early midwestern wool manufacturers is fragmentary, although material is available on the early lives of thirty-five of them. Fortunately the mills they founded were well distributed throughout the eight states of the region. All indications suggest that these men constitute a representative sample of middlewestern millowners, and that from an examination of their activities one can generalize regarding the entire industry.[31]

A majority of the men studied were born in Ohio, New York, or the New England states in the 1830s, married there, and moved to the Middle West in the twenty years between 1850 and 1870. With the exception of the six men born in foreign countries, migration to the region represented for most the first

30. For example, of Missouri's seventeen woolen mills in 1860, all were located in counties with a population of at least five thousand, and two-thirds were in counties of ten thousand or more people. Only two, however, were located in large cities (St. Joseph and St. Louis), and except for three mills in the northwest corner of the state, all were built at distances of approximately forty to fifty miles apart.

31. *Textile Manufacturers' Directory* (New York, 1883), listed 345 midwestern millowners whose names were then checked in various newspapers, county histories, and state and national biographical directories. In some cases, material on one individual was acquired from numerous sources.

major move away from the immediate locality of their place of birth.

Several pioneer woolen producers, at some time in their careers, had gained firsthand experience in some aspects of textile manufacturing. George Buell, who with the financial aid of his father, constructed a small woolen factory at St. Joseph, Missouri, in 1852, had managed a woolen mill in Illinois. Thomas Hainsworth was employed as foreman of an Indiana woolen firm before he established his own factory at Neosho, Missouri, in 1869, while Elisha Cockefair, who developed the Eagle Mills near Indianapolis, had acquired knowledge of production processes during his childhood apprenticeship to a weaver. W. W. Webster, founder of the Rushford, Minnesota, Woolen Mill in the late 1860s, had previously worked in his father's woolen factory at La Crescent, Minnesota. Typical of many cases, Waltus Watkins and Carl Klemer, who built woolen plants near Lawson, Missouri, and at Faribault, Minnesota, operated custom-carding machines prior to their attempts at the full-scale manufacture of fabrics.

For those millowners who possessed no previous knowledge of cloth fabrication, employment of skilled personnel proved essential. Midwestern mills sought qualified superintendents within the region to compensate for the lack of experience on the part of owners. For example, when F. J. Harwood and associates, who apparently had no prior connection with textiles, purchased Hutchinson and Company, a woolen factory in Appleton, Wisconsin, the new owners quickly retained the services of H. L. Waldo, Hutchinson's seasoned plant manager.[32] Manufacturers in the Middle West also attempted to hire superintendents from eastern factories to oversee production.

Like many pioneer promoters, several midwestern wool manufacturers pursued other economic activities in addition to retailing and wholesaling their cloth and yarn. Pliny S. Lyman, for example, not only produced woolens at his Corunna, Mich-

32. *Historical Review of the State of Wisconsin: Its Industrial and Commercial Resources* (New York, 1887), 78.

igan, mill, but manufactured bricks and carried on extensive farming operations.[33] Both Waltus Watkins and William Elliot owned sawmills and held stock in coal mines, while W. W. Hutchinson, Edward DeGarmo, Jefferson Benner, and Oren Stone all engaged in the dry goods business.[34] William James built a woolen factory at St. James, Missouri, in 1867, in addition to his investments in a flour mill and the Maramec Iron Works.[35]

Although several millowners had gained previous training in textile production, these men constituted a minority of those who constructed and operated woolen factories. Thus it seems obvious that in the Middle West, the venture into wool manufacturing merely represented an attempt to reap profits from one of a large number of business enterprises, and that the investment in woolen mills did not indicate a special commitment or attachment to that one particular industry. This is further illustrated by the fact that many invested capital in trade and in other types of manufacturing. Therefore, typical of a developing region, midwestern wool manufacturers appear to have been opportunity-oriented rather than industry-oriented.[36]

Since at least thirteen of the sample had previously been merchants or were the sons of merchants, mercantile capital provided a portion of the funds to finance midwestern wool manufacturing. Perhaps more significant, however, at some time in the past, nearly one-half of the sample group had risked capital in some other type of manufacturing, including barrel

33. Personal Diary of Pliny S. Lyman, Corunna Woolen Manufacturer, Pliny S. Lyman Papers, in the Michigan Historical Collections, University of Michigan, Ann Arbor.

34. Watkins (Watkins Mill, Lawson, Missouri); Elliot (Elliot Woolen Mill, St. Catherine, Missouri); DeGarmo (Warrensburg Woolen Mill, Warrensburg, Missouri); Hutchinson (Appleton Woolen Mills, Appleton, Wisconsin); Benner (Rockford Woolen Mill, Rockford, Minnesota); Stone (Stone-Atwood Company, Flint, Michigan).

35. James D. Norris, *Frontier Iron: The Maramec Iron Works 1826–1876* (Madison, Wis., 1964), 155.

36. For a brief discussion of opportunity orientation, see "Investing in Modern Management: The 'free-form' Corporation," Equity Research Associates, *Bulletin,* September 20, 1966, p. 9.

and paper factories, flour mills, meatpacking plants, and wagon works. Moreover, several had owned sawmills and a few had speculated in land. Only two had previously farmed and only one person could be considered a skilled artisan. Thus, profits acquired directly from earlier business enterprises in large part financed construction and production in the early woolen mills of the Middle West.

In his study of fifty-seven businessmen in Illinois between 1820 and 1890, Donald Kemmerer discovered that borrowing or inheritance proved unimportant in providing funds for beginning manufacturing plants in that state. Since most pioneer enterprises required relatively small amounts of money, many Illinois businessmen had acquired sufficient capital in previous pursuits, such as merchandising, to commence operation.[37] However, because factory production of woolens required a large building, complicated and expensive machinery, skilled labor, and a raw material inventory, it necessitated a larger monetary outlay than the ordinary pioneer manufacturing venture. The Middle West's 881 woolen mills in 1870 represented an average capital investment of approximately $17,700; in that same year, the average investment in these factories exceeded the average capital investment in the midwestern manufacture of boots and shoes, bricks, carriages and wagons, pumps, saddles and harnesses, tanned leather, and the packing of meat.[38]

Pioneer woolen men needed larger capital resources than some manufacturers, but they lacked a pool of investment funds within the Middle West from which to draw. The immobility of capital among regions of the United States hindered economic growth throughout most of the nineteenth century, and although western interest rates generally remained higher than those on the eastern market, savers in the East were often

37. Donald L. Kemmerer, "Financing Illinois Industry, 1830–1890," *Bulletin of the Business Historical Society* 27 (June 1953): 110. Only one of the fifty-seven businessmen studied by Kemmerer was a wool manufacturer.
38. U.S. Department of Commerce, Bureau of the Census, *Census of Manufactures: 1905, Textiles, Bulletin 74*, 134–36.

reluctant to risk large sums in western manufacturing enterprises. Mobility within an industry usually took place only when investors migrated west taking their capital with them.[39] Therefore, a few middlewestern manufacturers experienced difficulty raising money for initial woolen mill construction.

Although the town of Reedsburg, Wisconsin, dispatched agents to New York in the 1850s to solicit funds for a mill, local citizens had to await the arrival of eastern investors who moved there.[40] And, following his failure to secure loans in Missouri in 1860, Waltus Watkins found it necessary to enlist financial support from family members and friends in Kentucky in order to continue construction and begin operation of his new woolen factory.[41] As late as 1892, the owners of the Faribault Woolen Mill in Minnesota could not collect enough capital from Faribault citizens to rebuild the factory following a fire in September of that year.[42] Those mills which escaped the pinch of scarcity during their formative period often turned to incorporation when funds were needed to expand operations. As only a few examples, woolen factories in Minneapolis, Minnesota; Fulton, Missouri; Clinton, Michigan; and Appleton, Beaver Dam, Cedarburg, and Racine, Wisconsin, all incorporated between 1866 and 1883.[43]

39. Lance E. Davis, "Capital Immobilities and Finance Capitalism: A Study of Economic Evolution in the United States, 1820–1890," *Explorations in Entrepreneurial History*, vol. 1, 2d ser. (Fall 1963): 88–96. Exceptions did exist. For example, meatpacking, a western industry which marketed substantial portions of its output in the East, received capital from eastern investors. See Rudolf A. Clemen, *The American Livestock and Meat Industry* (New York, 1923), 137.

40. Merton E. Krug, *History of Reedsburg and the Upper Baraboo Valley* (Madison, Wis., 1929), 36; William H. Canfield, *Outline Sketches of Sauk County* (Baraboo, Wis., 1872), 22–23.

41. Mary Handy to Waltus Watkins, Mercer County, Kentucky, September 24 and December 2, 1869, and promissory note, Waltus Watkins to Jane Watkins, April 11, 1862, in the private collection of Mrs. Manfred Weber, Shawnee Mission, Kansas.

42. Frank H. Klemer, "The History of the Faribault Woolen Mills" (paper read before the Rice County, Minnesota, Historical Society, October 22, 1940, copy in the Minnesota Historical Society, St. Paul).

43. Of course, incorporation could have indicated an attempt by a millowner to unload a bad investment. However, extant company records indicate that in most cases capital acquired through incorporation financed expansion programs.

In many cases midwestern woolen mills were family operations and an examination of company records indicates a high
degree of nepotism. Major administrative positions in woolen
mills at Lawson and St. Joseph, Missouri; Faribault, La Crescent, Minneapolis, and Rushford, Minnesota; and Lacon, Illinois, were dominated by relatives of owners and managers. The
1884 corporate minutes of the Appleton Mills in Wisconsin
illustrate a typical case where three members of the same
family were president, general manager, and secretary-treas-
urer.[44]

Given such a situation, relatives frequently assumed control
of a firm upon the death or retirement of the original owner, or,
after several years with the mill, withdrew from the company
and established a similar factory in another locality. For example, when Isaac Chapman, owner of the Watertown, Wisconsin,
woolen mill died in 1885, his wife Jane continued to operate the
business for some time,[45] and the three sons of Waltus Watkins
manufactured cloth and yarn for several years after their father's retirement in the mid-1880s. Edward McFetridge and his
brother James built the Beaver Dam, Wisconsin, Woolen Mill in
1866. Nine years later James sold his interest in the plant in
order to buy into the Island Woolen Mills at Baraboo, Wisconsin.[46]

The numerous steps in the fabrication of woolen cloth multi-
plied the different types of machinery required for its production. Since they had located in a relatively unpopulated region,
those manufacturers who built woolen mills in the Middle West
prior to 1870 found it necessary to order equipment from many
different firms scattered throughout the United States. The
Watkins Mill, which operated from 1861 to 1886, bought its
boiler from a St. Louis foundry, spindles and cards from Philadelphia, and weaving appliances from loomworks in New Jer-

44. Appleton Mills, Corporate Minutes, Director's Meeting, January 10, 1884, in the possession of the company, Appleton, Wisconsin.

45. *Historical Review of the State of Wisconsin*, 136.

46. *Memorial and Genealogical Record of Dodge and Jefferson
Counties, Wisconsin* (Chicago, 1894), 17.

sey.[47] Although textile machine manufacturers had agents in Indianapolis and other midwestern cities by 1860, most mill-owners had to await the arrival of materials from eastern concerns. As late as 1874, when the owners of the Appleton Mills ordered machinery from a woolen manufacturer's supply house in Milwaukee, they discovered that the Milwaukee firm did not build or stock such equipment but merely accepted advance orders for an eastern company.[48]

Since they operated where knowledge of complicated textile equipment was limited, midwestern wool manufacturers frequently relied on machine builders for the installation of new appliances. For example, J. T. Dewdall and Company of St. Louis, manufacturer of the boiler for the Watkins Mill, sent their own engineer to northwest Missouri in the fall of 1860 to install the engine, boiler, and its connective apparatus.[49] And, in December 1893, the Buell Manufacturing Company, a woolen mill in St. Joseph, Missouri, requested that the C. G. Sargent Company send a man from the factory at Graniteville, Massachusetts, to unpack and set up their new wool dryer.[50]

Although machinery suppliers were miles to the east, mid-western manufacturers enjoyed a close proximity to raw wool supplies. As early as the 1840s eastern farmers started to abandon sheep raising, and the Merino flocks of New England and the Middle Atlantic moved into Ohio and then spread over the other states of the Middle West. The relocation of sheep to the center of the continent necessitated some major alterations in the structure of the domestic wool market.

47. J. T. Dewdall and Company, St. Louis, November 26, 1860, August 8, 1860, February 21, 1861, Alfred Jenks and Son, Philadelphia, January 1, 1861, and Van Ripper and Son, Patterson, April 8, 1869, March 18, 1869, to Watkins Mill, in the Watkins Mill Collection, Jackson County, Missouri, Historical Society Archives, Independence.

48. Northwestern Woolen Manufacturers's Supply House to Appleton Mills, Milwaukee, August 22, 1874, in the Appleton Mills Collection, State Historical Society of Wisconsin, Madison.

49. E. N. Dewdall to Watkins Mill, St. Louis, October 31, 1860, in the Watkins Collection.

50. C. G. Sargent Company to The Buell Manufacturing Company, Graniteville, December 15, 1893, in the C. G. Sargent Collection, Merrimack Valley Textile Museum, North Andover, Massachusetts.

CHAPTER III

The Marketing of Wool
in the Middle West

Sheep moved westward with each advance of settlers, and as small farms filled the Middle West after 1850, woolgrowing became an important aspect of the region's economy. With expansion of the eastern woolen textile industry, midwestern farmers found in wool a commodity which could withstand transport charges over long distances. Within a few years, both eastern and western businessmen established permanent wool-houses in the region, many local produce traders specialized in wool, agents of eastern woolen mills made annual visits to the Middle West to procure raw material, and a host of rural storekeepers accepted wool from farmers in payment of accounts. By 1870, the thirteen million sheep on midwestern farms provided fleece in sufficient quantities to generate the formation of a widespread, yet relatively inefficient, system of wool marketing.[1]

Thanks to the importation of large numbers of foreign breeding rams during the mania for Merinos[2] after 1801, and an 1820 speculation in Saxony sheep, a Merino type, the quality of American wool slowly improved.[3] In response to the high fleece prices of the 1820s, many eastern farmers adopted woolgrowing, and, as a result, the American sheep population doubled between 1814 and 1831. In the latter year, New York, Pennsylvania, and Vermont contained large portions of the estimated twenty million sheep in the United States.[4]

While eastern farmers sought to meet the demand of the textile industry for raw material, businessmen in the major port cities organized commission houses which specialized in buying and selling wool. Throughout most of the antebellum period,

Boston triumphed over New York and Philadelphia as the nation's major wool market, and the city retained its dominant position long after the exodus of sheep from the Northeast. As late as 1870, Boston's wooldealers still handled 40 percent of the domestic clip.[5]

As northeastern cities spawned more and more woolhouses, cloth manufacturers combined fleece purchases from local farmers with orders to these firms in an effort to acquire correct grades and quantities of wool. In the mid-1830s, Faulkner and Colony, a woolen factory at Keene, New Hampshire, bought most of its wool directly from farmers and country storekeepers. However, by 1856 the mill also utilized the services of wooldealers throughout New England.[6] And, in the 1860s, the Agawam

1. U.S. Department of Commerce, Bureau of the Census, Eleventh Census, *Agriculture: 1890*, 92–93.

2. There are four major classifications of sheep: the Merino, a Spanish development, which produces a fine, greasy fleece; English breeds, exhibiting long, coarse wool, and possessing a larger carcass than the Merino; the crossbreeds, composed of various Merino-English crosses; and the native sheep of all countries, whose coarse wool is not normally satisfactory for cloth production. American Sheep Producers Council, *Breeds of Sheep*, Educational Pamphlet 3 (Denver, Colo., n.d.), passim.

3. Discussions of the Merino Mania and subsequent sheep crazes can be found in Carroll W. Pursell, Jr., "E. I. Dupont and the Merino Mania in Delaware, 1805–1815," *Agricultural History* 26 (April 1962): 91–100, and "E. I. Dupont, Don Pedro, and the Introduction of Merino Sheep into the United States, 1801: A Document," *Agricultural History* 33 (April 1959): 86–88; Arthur Harrison Cole, "Agricultural Crazes," *American Economic Review* 16 (December 1926): 622–39.

4. U.S., Congress, Senate, *The Wool Trade of the United States*, 61st Cong., 1st sess., Senate Misc. Doc. 70, p. 41; L. G. Connor, "A Brief History of the Sheep Industry in the United States," American Historical Association, *Report* 1 (1918): 109–10.

5. U.S. Bureau of Statistics, *Wool and Manufactures of Wool* (Washington, D.C., 1888), lxvi–lxvii; George H. Gibson, "The Growth of the Woolen Industry in Nineteenth Century Delaware," *Textile History Review* 5 (October 1964): 131; *The Wool Trade of the United States*, 30–31, 42–52.

6. Incoming Correspondence, 1836, and D. B. Sexton to Faulkner and Colony, Cleveland, May 10, 1856, in the Faulkner and Colony Collection, Manuscripts Division, Baker Library, Harvard University.

Woolen Company, in Massachusetts, procured fleece through purchases from area woolgrowers, in addition to buying from several Boston commission merchants.[7]

Direct buying saved millowners the fee charged by woolhouses, but large factories soon discovered that local flocks were usually incapable of meeting raw material needs. Therefore, mills placed heavy dependence upon wooldealers to supply them. In the early years of his business, Nathaniel Stevens bought wool from farmers in the immediate vicinity of his factory in Andover, Massachusetts. By 1830, a representative of the firm toured Maine, Vermont, and New Hampshire visiting shearing pens and contracting for fleece from woolgrowers and dealers. However, except for an occasional trip to the Far West, the Stevens Company appears to have abandoned direct purchases by 1860, preferring instead to depend upon wool merchants to supply the mill with the bulk of raw material.[8]

Sheep continued to move west with each advancing line of settlement. Merinos entered the Zanesville, Ohio, area as early as 1801, and by 1820 some settlements in Illinois and Indiana had received large numbers of sheep. In spite of these initial gains, in most western states woolgrowing made little commercial progress prior to 1830. Sheep were heavily concentrated in some areas, but household manufacturing usually absorbed substantial portions of fleece output. As only one example, all but approximately 8 percent of Washington County, Pennsylvania's, 1825 clip of 400,000 pounds was consumed locally.[9]

7. For examples, see letters from Massachusetts farmers and storekeepers in Beckett, November 20, 1866, West Springfield, October 15, 1866, and Enfield, August 3, 1866, to Agawam Woolen Company, in the Merrimack Valley Textile Museum, North Andover, Massachusetts.

8. Nathaniel Stevens and Son, Wool Bills, July 13, 1859–January 6, 1870, in the Merrimack Valley Textile Museum, North Andover, Massachusetts; Horace Stevens, *Nathaniel Stevens, 1786–1865* (North Andover, Mass., 1946), 29–30, 62–63; Nathaniel Stevens, *Early Days of the Woolen Industry in North Andover, Massachusetts: A Sketch* (North Andover, Mass., 1925), 20–21.

9. Percy W. Bidwell and John I. Falconer, *History of Agriculture in the Northern United States, 1620–1860* (New York, 1941), 183.

Completion of the Erie Canal in 1825 expanded the volume of wool moving eastward, and twenty years later it was estimated that over two million pounds cleared Buffalo bound for tidewater.[10] Through canal construction and river improvement, Illinois and Indiana joined Ohio and Pennsylvania in developing direct eastern market connections in the early fifties. And by 1853 railroads linked St. Louis, Chicago, and the Great Lakes Region to the Atlantic Coast. The seemingly endless quantities of western fleece pouring into seaboard markets forced many northeastern farmers to abandon sheep raising. From 1850 to 1860 woolgrowers in areas comprising New York and New England thinned flocks by 63 percent.[11]

High value per pound and durability supported heavy freight charges for wool over long distances, and the favorable transport costs for wool as compared to other agricultural commodities prompted many midwestern farmers to buy sheep. Around 1840, one pound of high grade wool would carry twenty pounds to market, while the fifty-seven cent differential between New York and Chicago wheat prices amply illustrated the high freight rates for grain.[12] As late as 1862, J. B. Grinnell, an Iowa farmer, succinctly stated the situation: "I give 80 percent of the value of my wheat which impoverishes my farm, to find a market; and 4 percent to find the best wool market."[13]

Two other factors helped to promote middlewestern woolgrowing. Since sheep were relatively easy to turn to, grain farmers could periodically reallocate capital from cereals to wool, and the low agricultural prices of the early 1840s encouraged such investments. Second, the milder winters in the south-

10. U.S., Congress, Senate, Israel D. Andrews, *Trade and Commerce of the British North American Colonies, and upon the Great Lakes and Rivers,* 1854, 32d Cong., 1st sess., Senate Exec. Doc. 112, p. 92.

11. Harold F. Wilson, "The Rise and Decline of the Sheep Industry in Northern New England," *Agricultural History* 9 (January 1935): 20–21.

12. Connor, "Brief History of the Sheep Industry," 114–15.

13. As quoted in the *Report of the Commissioner of Agriculture,* 1862, U.S., Congress, House, 37th Cong., 3d sess., House Exec. Doc. 78, p. 304.

ern portions of the Middle West eliminated expensive feeding and shelter so necessary throughout New England from November through March. In 1862, Iowa sheepmen calculated their annual upkeep expenses at $0.75 to $1.00, while New York woolgrowers expended $2.00 per animal. And, following the Civil War, it was estimated that a Missouri farmer could keep a flock of sheep for one-half the cost of his New England counterpart.[14]

Some eastern sheepmen moved west. For example, Truman and Isaac Harvey established a sheep farm near La Salle, Illinois, in 1843 after migrating from Vermont. Enroute they purchased 2,300 animals in Columbus, Ohio, and to defray expenses, sold all but 1,200 on arrival in Illinois. Subsequent acquisitions of breeding rams from Vermont and Ohio aided flock improvement. The Harveys followed a typical approach by leasing some of their sheep to local farmers, with the lessee receiving either one-half the wool or lamb increase.[15] Henry Ancrum, a Pike County, Missouri, farmer suggested a slightly different plan when he advertised for sheep in 1849. Ancrum proposed to retain all the fleece and lambs, and to pay the owner 10 percent of the flock's annually assessed value.[16]

The center of American sheep production rapidly shifted westward after 1840. The phenomenal growth of sheep raising in Ohio and Michigan during the twenty years before 1860 represented only extreme examples of a common trend throughout the Middle West. By 1870, Indiana, Illinois, Michigan, and Ohio ranked among the top six wool-producing states.[17] The

14. Ibid., 303; Finla G. Crawford, "The Wool Industry of the United States, 1865–1870" (M.A. thesis, University of Wisconsin, 1916), 73; Ezra A. Carman, H. A. Heath, and John Minto, *Special Report on the History and Present Condition of the Sheep Industry of the United States* (Washington, D.C., 1892), 825.

15. U.S., Congress, House, *Report of the Commissioner of Patents, Agriculture,* 1845, 29th Cong., 1st sess., House Doc. 140, pp. 341–42.

16. *The Western Journal of Agriculture, Manufactures, Mechanic Arts, Internal Improvement, Commerce, and General Literature* 2 (February 1849): 131.

17. Armour's Livestock Bureau, *Monthly Letter to Animal Husbandmen* 13 (March 1935): 3.

general trade position of larger midwestern cities assured them of an active wool market once the region's sheep population became sufficiently dense to provide a commercial surplus. In the initial years of the trade, interior city wool merchants merely collected small lots for direct forwarding to Boston, Philadelphia, and New York. However, as fine-wooled Merinos continued to enter the Middle West, such cities as Chicago, Cleveland, Detroit, Kansas City, Milwaukee, and St. Louis represented important wool markets in their own right.

It soon became apparent to woolgrowers and manufacturers alike that the midwestern trade in wool constituted a highly imperfect market. That is, both buyers and sellers experienced unusual difficulty in finding efficient systems of purchase or sale. Many factors accounted for the imperfect nature of the market, yet nearly all causes of market inefficiency stemmed from the interaction of three major problem areas: (1) the inherent nature of wool, (2) the physical distribution of supply relative to the locus of demand, and (3) inadequate communications between buyer and seller in the marketplace.

The unique characteristics of wool in part shaped the structure of the market created to handle it. The major properties which determined wool value were its fineness, length and strength, color, sheen and softness, and the volume of foreign material imbedded in the fibers. Moreover, wool might differ as much as 30 to 80 percent in shrinkage, or the loss in weight when it was scoured in a warm alkali solution to remove impurities. These qualities varied among breeds, regions, flocks, seasons of the year, within a single fleece, and yearly within the same locality. There were over two thousand grades of raw wool and as many as thirteen of these might be sorted from the wool of one animal. Thus, each fleece constituted a unique product which inhibited the standardization of grades and the formation of a futures market.[18]

18. Benjamin Richards, *Textiles* (New York, 1939), 8; the New York Wool Top Exchange was not established until 1931. Wool "top," or the combed and drawn fibers used in worsted production, could be standardized and, therefore, allowed the development of futures

As sheep continued to leave the Northeast, inadequate market information plagued both the grower and manufacturer of wool. In the Middle West, a multitude of persons, scattered over a broad geographic area, raised sheep as part of a general farming program. Numerous factors, ranging from the weather to the market price of other agricultural commodities, affected the quantity and quality of the wool clip. Therefore, each spring woolen manufacturers and farmers attempted to predict what grades and quantities of fleece would be available during the summer and fall, and at what prices they would be bought and sold.

Although cloth producers enjoyed a relatively constant demand throughout the year, most wool went to market immediately after shearing. Also, maintaining a large wool inventory required storage facilities and tied up capital. The high shrinkage rate of most Merino wools offered an additional danger since a miscalculation in weight could mean the difference between profit and loss. Each type of fabric required a different combination of wool grades, yet most eastern textile mills found it necessary to bid on wool prior to the establishment of prices and fashions in the cloth market. Unlike cotton factories, the absence of a futures market in raw wool prohibited woolen mills from hedging to reduce the risks of price increases on raw material.

To many woolgrowers the problem seemed equally complex. They faced several alternative methods of sale in a market where prices usually fluctuated in response to changes in supply and demand. Yet except in their immediate neighborhoods, ignorance of the quantity offered for sale and quality of other wool on the market limited the number of rational choices. The lack of a few standard grade classifications prevented most farmers from comparing the prices offered for local

trading. However, wool top constituted a semimanufactured product. For a discussion of the organization and operation of the New York Wool Top Exchange, consult Alston Hill Garside, *Wool and the Wool Trade* (New York, 1939), 103–47, and Paul T. Cherington, "Some Aspects of the Wool Trade of the United States," *Quarterly Journal of Economics* 25 (February 1911): 337–56.

wool with quotations in other markets. To help maximize his profits from woolgrowing the farmer had to decide whether to sell at the shearing pen, to a wool dealer or local trader, ship fleece directly to the eastern market or consign it to a commission merchant there, store it hoping for a price advance, or to dispose of his clip through any number of other market outlets.

Perceiving the high degree of imperfection, many middlemen entered the wool market hoping to capitalize on the uncertainties of the trade and to reap profits from the purchase and sale of fleece. The marketing of wool in the Middle West, therefore, rapidly became a speculative operation composed of many small buyers and sellers. Aside from their functions as buyers and shippers, wool dealers could have provided an important link between farmers and manufacturers in the passage of information. However, most chose to keep woolgrowers uninformed and thereby hoped to purchase fleece at relatively low prices.

Concentration of the wool clip at a few convenient locations offered one possible solution to the farmer's ignorance of the total market. And the Middle West gave birth to the first wool pool, organized in Greencastle, Indiana, in 1855. Pooling concentrated the wool of many growers for sale to the highest bidder, and this method of marketing assumed increasing importance following the Civil War. Since they normally existed only while the clip was being sold, pools should not be confused with farm cooperatives. Rather than tightly controlled cooperation, pools operated as loosely structured local farm organizations providing only temporary central markets and giving dealers and eastern mill agents easy access to area wool. In most of the early pools, sorting and grading were not attempted, since farmers seemingly preferred to sell individual clips separately.[19]

Pools seldom satisfied both buyer and seller. Manufacturers

19. O. B. Jesness and W. H. Kerr, *Cooperative Purchasing and Marketing Organizations among Farmers in the United States,* United States Department of Agriculture, Bulletin 547, p. 1; Deane W. Malott and Boyce F. Martin, *The Agricultural Industries* (New York, 1939), 412–13; A. F. DuPlessis, *The Marketing of Wool* (London, 1931), 200–201.

argued that in an advancing market farmers ignored the pool, and either sold direct to local speculators or consigned wool to commission merchants. Falling prices prompted farmers to enter a pool, and many deemed it the duty of manufacturers to take all the wool offered. In the larger pools, buyers sometimes graded clips, but were closely watched by farmers, and should woolen men sort fleeces too carefully, the pool might refuse to sell to them in the future. Woolgrowers, on the other hand, bitterly complained of buyer secrecy and collusion.[20] Farmers suspected that through a prearranged agreement, bidders intentionally offered low prices for the first few lots auctioned, hoping thereby to create the impression that a surplus of fleece existed throughout the region.[21]

During the infant years of factory production, eastern woolen millowners sometimes found it necessary to maintain their own flocks in order to provide enough high-quality fleece. However, as both the quantity and quality of American wool increased after 1820, most factories abandoned woolgrowing and procured raw material through face-to-face contacts with farmers. Almost from the first movement of sheep into the Middle West, eastern woolen manufacturers sent their buying agents in pursuit of fleece. For example, the agents of Lowell factory owners were purchasing wool in the Edgerton, Ohio, area as early as 1847, and a large portion of the Clinton County, Indiana, 1854 wool clip went to buyers who represented eastern mills.[22]

Many woolgrowers distrusted agent buyers, but lacking sufficient knowledge of the market, the growers sometimes depended upon them to purchase fleece. If the farmer consigned his wool to an eastern commission merchant, he shouldered

20. Copy of "An Interview, Lucile Kane with William G. Northup in the Minneapolis Offices of the North Star Woolen Mills," November 16, 1949, in the Minnesota Historical Society, St. Paul.

21. Harry James Brown, "The National Association of Wool Manufacturers, 1864–1897" (Ph.D. diss., Cornell University, 1948), provides an excellent description of grower-manufacturer conflicts.

22. U.S., Congress, House, *Report of the Commissioner of Patents for the Year 1853*, 33d Cong., 1st sess., House Exec. Doc. 39, p. 40; *Niles' National Register* 72 (July 24, 1847), 331.

part of the capital burden and ran the risk of falling prices.[23] Choosing the best eastern wool dealer provided an annual frustration, as illustrated by Sam Boardman, a farmer near Lincoln, Illinois. In 1868, Boardman sarcastically counseled a sheep raiser on the proper method to employ in selecting an eastern wool commission merchant; the farmer should "get the best information he can with regard to different wool houses, shut his eyes, and send it."[24]

Other than eastern mill buyers, pooling, and consigned shipment, midwestern woolgrowers also sold directly to local traders, who purchased wool as one of a number of items in general speculative trading. The local resident trader usually bought and sold any item which promised a quick profit and rapid capital turnover. As fleece supplies increased in the Middle West, some local traders specialized in wool. For example, Lothrop Johnson, a local trader, purchased wool on his own account in Gainesville, Michigan, from 1859 to 1864. He spent several thousand dollars each spring for wool ranging from quantities as small as one fleece to several thousand pounds. Johnson apparently bought all grades of wool since in early 1859 he paid prices which varied from $0.20 to $0.62 per pound. The scarcity of wool during the Civil War, however, forced him to offer as much as $1.00 per pound in 1864.[25]

After 1850, several eastern woolhouses flooded the Middle West with agents before and during the clipping season to collect lots directly from farmers or local traders. For example,

23. On wool consignments, commission merchants usually extended cash advances to farmers at the rate of two-thirds to three-fourths of the estimated market value of the fleece. However, woolgrowers often paid 6 percent interest for such advances in addition to a selling commission. Robert L. Studley, "The Marketing and Financing of Wool" (an address delivered before the Robert Morris Associates, Boston, November 17, 1923, copy in the Baker Library, Harvard University).

24. As quoted in the Missouri State Board of Agriculture, *Report,* 1868, 136.

25. Lothrop Johnson, Wool Purchase Book, Gainesville, Michigan, 1859–1864, in the Michigan Historical Collections, University of Michigan, Ann Arbor.

Sutliff and Case, wool merchants of Cleveland, Ohio, sent Nathan Brownell, Jr., to Michigan in the early spring of 1851
under instructions to establish a purchasing agency in Detroit.[26]
The parent firm channeled capital through Brownell, to local
buyers, during April and May.[27] Brownell's buyers in turn supplied their side agents with funds to purchase for Sutliff and
Case. Local agents examined wool, made the purchase, and
arranged for sacking and transit, usually receiving a commission of one cent per pound. In the Detroit area alone, Brownell
released over $42,000 for wool purchases during the 1851 sea-
son.[28] Although this method dispersed capital and agents
throughout the wool area and aided in procuring the clip, it also
reduced communications among buyers in a highly unpredictable market where knowledge of day-to-day price changes
proved imperative.

Brownell relayed instructions that buyers should begin bidding at last-season prices to test the market. As the buying
progressed, Sutliff and Case warned Brownell of the shaky
nature of the eastern wool market, and suggested that he lower
bids to conform to the situation.[29] Concern quickly produced
criticism. Early July found Sutliff and Case angrily instructing
Brownell to withdraw funds from local buyers until they followed instructions, because, from their vantage point in Cleveland, it appeared to them that "Michigan was the worst place to
purchase wool there is in the western states."[30] Throughout
August, Sutliff and Case carefully observed prices in the eastern
cloth trade and, as they continued to fall, impressed upon
Brownell the urgency of withholding his Michigan agents from

26. Sutliff and Case to Nathan Brownell, Jr., Cleveland, April 18,
1851, Nathan Brownell, Jr., Papers, in the Michigan Historical Collections, University of Michigan, Ann Arbor.

27. Sutliff and Case to Brownell, Cleveland, May 3, 5, 11, 1851,
Brownell Papers.

28. Daniel Houskins to Brownell, Jackson, Michigan, May 7, 1851,
Brownell Papers.

29. Sutliff and Case to Brownell, Cleveland, June 6, 7, 1851,
Brownell Papers.

30. Ibid., July 10, 1851, Brownell Papers.

45

purchases.[31] Brownell's buyers complained.[32] Buck Thompson of Ann Arbor advised Brownell that competition from other dealers in that town had inflated prices three to five cents above the level he was directed to offer. Since he was an area resident and local trader, farmers expected him to bid on their wool; if he failed to do so, his reputation would suffer. If Brownell continued to maintain a noncompetitive bidding level, Thompson threatened to purchase wool on his own account.[33]

Purchasing agents like Brownell normally remained in a region only during the buying season. However, after 1860 some commission men established permanent woolhouses in many areas of the Middle West where the sheep population merited their existence. Such was the case when Thomas McGraw organized his Detroit woolhouse in April 1864, and six years later created a Boston branch office. McGraw migrated from Canada to Michigan with his father in 1835, and his early business training included bookkeeping, clerking for the Pittsburgh Iron Company, and operating a general store in Novi, Michigan.

Like several other dealers, McGraw first entered the wool trade by accepting fleece from farmers in payment of accounts at his store. In a short time his wool operations completely overshadowed all other business, and in 1864 he abandoned the mercantile aspect and moved to Detroit. In 1887 McGraw's wool purchases amounted to approximately five million pounds. He later became the major stockholder of the Globe Tobacco Company, president of the Michigan Savings Bank, and director of the American National Bank, all of Detroit.[34]

Typical of most agencies, Thomas McGraw and Company employed one or two permanent buyers who ranged over a wide

31. Ibid., August 23, 1851, Brownell Papers.
32. Daniel Houskins, Jackson, Michigan, May 28, 1851, H. Rexford, Ypsilanti, Michigan, May 20, 1851, and C. M. Brewer, Marshall, Michigan, June 3, 1851, to Brownell, Brownell Papers.
33. Buck Thompson to Brownell, Ann Arbor, May 28, 1851, Brownell Papers.
34. Silas Farmer, *The History of Detroit and Michigan* (Detroit, Mich., 1889), 1159–60.

geographic area in search of fleece. Such individuals often handled the allocation of funds among local buyers who purchased for McGraw on a commission of one cent per pound. To name only a few, during the 1865 shearing season McGraw had buyers who bid on local wool in the Michigan towns of Albion, Ann Arbor, Battle Creek, Dexter, Farmington, Flint, Ionia, Jackson, Lansing, Marshall, and Pontiac.[35]

After noting local trade activity and checking the prices offered by other dealers, McGraw's buyers called on area farmers, examined the wool, and placed bids. Since wool could sometimes be purchased cheaply if farmers were kept in ignorance of current prices, McGraw's local buyers seldom embarked on a program of market education. For example, E. B. Tyler, a McGraw buyer in Dexter, Michigan, wrote in June 1865 that "I keep cool—not anxious, letting the farmers have their own way, they are kind of up a stump, they know not what to do."[36] Tyler also cautioned McGraw to "make no one any offer that comes from here," since one Dexter farmer, who obviously did not trust Tyler, was journeying to Detroit to check the market and might seek a bid from McGraw personally.[37] In addition to his own agents, McGraw acquired wool through other channels. To fill an order in November 1864 he purchased fleece worth over $8,000 from Traugott Schmidt, a fellow Detroit wool dealer. E. S. Noble of Albion was only one of a host of country storekeepers who bought for McGraw, and the Ypsilanti woolen mill, like similar firms throughout Michigan, collected commissions by accepting fleece for McGraw's Detroit woolhouse.[38]

35. G. B. Johnson, Granville, Ohio, June 7, 24, and August 20, 1865, and N. P. Smith, Kensington, Michigan, June 18, 1865, to Thomas McGraw, in the Thomas McGraw Papers, Burton Historical Collection, Detroit Public Library, Detroit.

36. E. B. Tyler to McGraw, Dexter, Michigan, June 17, 1865, McGraw Papers.

37. Ibid., May 25, 1865, McGraw Papers.

38. Sales receipt, Traugott Schmidt, Detroit, November 23, 1864, and letters from E. S. Noble, Albion, Michigan, May 30, 1865, Ypsilanti Woolen Manufacturing Company, Ypsilanti, Michigan, June 2, 1865, to McGraw, McGraw Papers.

Before the establishment of his Massachusetts branch office, McGraw maintained a joint account with Nevins and Company, commission merchants in Boston. McGraw frequently purchased Michigan wools which were then forwarded to Nevins to fill an order, or were added to the Nevins-McGraw inventory. During the last two years of the Civil War, Nevins kept McGraw constantly informed on the changing price of gold since both firms apparently felt it offered the best barometer for predicting future business. In November 1864, Nevins advised McGraw that the market was "very dull. Wool is depressed and few sales taking place owing to the . . . uncertainty of gold."[39] Although rumors of peace circulated through some Boston business circles by late January 1865, McGraw was warned to avoid optimism since "gold fluctuates at 5% to 10% daily and things are very unsettled in trade."[40] At home in Michigan, McGraw found others concerned; a scarcity of bank currency plagued many areas, country banks often refused to cash drafts drawn on Detroit, and farmers demanded either greenbacks or national currency in payment for their wool.[41]

Following the Civil War McGraw expanded operations and by the late 1860s he represented the typical full-function market intermediary. His firm accepted wool consigned from growers, charging 1 to 2 percent sales commission, filled direct orders from other woolhouses, sold to eastern and western woolen mills, and sorted and stored fleece awaiting factory needs.[42] McGraw also advanced cash on wool consignments, discounted commercial paper, made direct loans, accepted personal notes, and sold to textile mills on credit ranging from a few days to several months. The Massachusetts branch office expedited

39. Nevins and Company to McGraw, Boston, November 21, 1864, McGraw Papers.

40. Ibid., January 30, 1865, McGraw Papers.

41. H. Stevens, Albion, Michigan, June 21, 1864, E. B. Tyler, Albion, Michigan, May 23, 1865, and Merrifield and Willer, Lansing, Michigan, June 16, 1865, to McGraw, McGraw Papers.

42. L. W. Blakesly, Aurora, Illinois, October 16, 1866, Bumh and Gray Company, Janesville, Michigan, May 2, 1870, and Chamberlin Brothers and Company, Boston, August 16, 1866, to McGraw, McGraw Papers.

wool sales, since samples of Detroit fleece could be relayed to the Boston warehouse for inspection by potential purchasers. To reduce expenses, McGraw arranged with a Michigan railroad for a "confidential" shipping rate, by agreeing to transport all his eastbound wool on their trains. The new freight charge of one cent per pound from Detroit to Boston represented a 50 percent saving.[43]

Not all wool merchants in the Middle West dealt directly with farmers. Mauger and Avery,[44] wool dealers of Boston with branch offices in Chicago, New York, Philadelphia, and Providence, acquired the major portion of their fleece from smaller commission houses throughout the country. Although the firm occasionally dispatched a buyer to the middlewestern shearing pens to search for a large lot, or to seek a special type of wool, Mauger and Avery preferred to buy from interior city dealers in Chicago, Detroit, Kansas City, Milwaukee, and St. Louis.[45]

Eastern woolen mills placed direct orders for fleece with Mauger and Avery, or asked to be contacted when a particular type of wool appeared on the market.[46] The home office in Boston coordinated ordering, buying, and sales, then relayed this information to all its branches. With most direct orders,

43. J. D. Hayes, Detroit, April 23, 1870, Gregory and Merrill Company, Pontiac, Michigan, June 12, 1869, Nevins and Company, Boston, October 7, 1870, Bank of Montreal, Hamilton, Ontario, November 16, 1870, Joseph J. Hedges, Constantine, Michigan, September 25, 1871, Chamberlin Brothers and Company, Boston, September 14, 1866, and J. P. Crawley, Morenci, Michigan, May 20, 1870, to McGraw, McGraw Papers.

44. The Mauger and Avery business records (M–A Collection) which cover the period 1873–1914, are on deposit in the Manuscripts Division, Baker Library, Harvard University. The collection contains some 249 volumes and ten cases of unbound materials.

45. For example, in the summer of 1885, Mauger and Avery sent a buyer as far west as Russell, Kansas, in search of wool. T. K. Hastings to Mauger and Avery, Russell, Kansas, July 7, 1885, M–A Collection.

46. As only one illustration, all Mauger and Avery branches in 1885 appeared to possess a standing order to purchase fleece for the George H. Gilbert Manufacturing Company of Ware, Massachusetts. H. W. Booth to Mauger and Avery, Chicago, March 11, 1885, M–A Collection.

buying was left to the wool merchant's discretion. If, however, the purchase involved a large sum of money, the eastern mill might send a representative to the wool to examine the entire lot.[47]

In the mid-1880s, H. W. Booth headed the Mauger and Avery office in Chicago. Booth handled the acquisition and shipment of the firm's midwestern wool purchases and filled fleece orders from the other Mauger and Avery branches. In addition to these duties, all offices of the firm depended upon Booth to provide them with relevant information on the movement of wool in the Middle West. Therefore, he periodically reported on the quantity, quality, and estimated price of wool held by dealers throughout the region. Booth carefully observed the actions of his competitors, attempted to determine their eastern customers, and then sent this information to Boston.[48] To assemble such material, he frequently traveled to Detroit, Milwaukee, and St. Louis and maintained a close correspondence with wool dealers in other cities. On occasion, Booth collected a 1 percent brokerage fee by arranging sales between small midwestern dealers and eastern manufacturers.[49]

The midwestern shearing season began in the spring, and might vary with climate from as early as April in Missouri, to mid-June in Minnesota. In addition to the larger shearing crews which advanced northward from Mexico in March, a few itinerant shearers, who worked alone, traveled at random through the region in search of sheep. Some farmers who kept small flocks in isolated areas sheared their own sheep, often extracting both mutton and wool from the poor animals. To solve the difficult problem of moving heavy wool wagons over muddy roads, some growers drove their sheep to the banks of the Illinois, Missouri,

47. Examples of the firm's sales methods can be seen in the correspondence to the Chicago office during the 1880s.
48. In writing to Boston in 1885 concerning the relocation of the Chicago office, Booth argued for one particular site since other wool merchants were close, and "they can be watched." H. W. Booth to Mauger and Avery, Chicago, March 11, 1885, M–A Collection.
49. Ibid., January 8, 1882, and January 13, 1885, M–A Collection.

Mississippi, and Ohio rivers and did their shearing adjacent to the transportation outlet.[50]

Most midwestern farmers washed their sheep before shearing, but a few woolgrowers simplified the process by driving them through shallow water a few days before the fleece was removed. In 1868, one Missouri farmer claimed that he washed sheep by "swimming them three times across a running stream, with an hour's interval between swims,"[51] which seemed to be a common formula. Even the process of washing each sheep by hand had little value, but because of tradition buyers continued to discount unwashed wool.[52]

A feeling of mutual distrust between buyer and seller permeated the midwestern wool market. In the minds of some woolgrowers, the methods employed by buyers justified a certain degree of dishonesty. In response to real and imagined exploitation, some farmers tied wool bundles with enormous quantities of heavy twine to add weight. One eastern manufacturer is said to have received 121 feet of jute rope along with his purchase of an Ohio fleece, and some woolsacks being readied for shipment received liberal injections of extraneous matter. Textile millowners screamed fraud and deception, but in most cases exact identification of guilty parties proved impossible. In turn, when manufacturers or commission merchants discounted what they considered to be excessively dirty wool, or fleece containing a high percentage of impurities, farmers became vehement.[53]

50. Edward Norris Wentworth, *America's Sheep Trails, History, Personalities* (Ames, Iowa, 1948), 77.

51. As quoted in the Missouri State Board of Agriculture, *Report,* 1868, 133.

52. For example, wool purchased by the North Star Woolen Mills of Minneapolis in February 1877 showed a five to six cent differential between washed and unwashed fleece. Wool Book, 1877–1881, in the North Star Woolen Mill Company Records, Minnesota Historical Society, St. Paul.

53. Wentworth, *America's Sheep Trails,* 575; Dominion of Canada, Department of Agriculture, *The Sheep Industry in Canada, Great Britain, and United States* (Ottawa, 1911), 52–53; National Association of Wool Manufacturers, *Bulletin* 28 (June 1908): 140–57.

Domestic production of wool lagged well behind domestic consumption throughout the last half of the nineteenth century.[54] Theoretically, this implies a seller's market with wool-growers reaping the benefits.[55] However, market imperfections, caused by the nature of the product, the geographic dispersion of woolgrowing, and poor channels of market communication reversed this advantage. Middlemen entering the trade recognized that the maximization of current and future profits depended upon close cooperation with manufacturers. Wool purchased at low prices in the Middle West meant higher profit margins when sold in the eastern market, and assured wool dealers that textile mills in the East would utilize their services in the future. Thus, in most years, buyers dominated the midwestern wool market.

Despite recognition of their plight, sheep raisers seemed unwilling or unable to alter the structure of the market. No single farmer produced wool in sufficient quantities to effect changes in price levels. And, since sheep represented only a small portion of the capital investment of most farmers, few could afford the time or money necessary to create an efficient regional or national organization to improve the marketing of wool. Such a body might have handled the concentration and sale of fleece, collected and disseminated relevant market information, and promoted better sheep husbandry. However, the immense number of wool grades and the dispersed nature of the industry stood as effective barriers in the path of change. County and state woolgrower associations sprang up throughout the Middle West, but such groups seemingly felt content to hold annual conventions characterized by rhetoric rather than action, and to

54. U.S. Department of Commerce, Bureau of the Census, *Census of Manufactures: 1905, Textiles, Bulletin 74,* 107.

55. This argument rests upon two assumptions: (1) most middle-western farmers sold their wool to buyers in the domestic market; (2) woolen textile manufacturers purchased the major portion of their raw material inside the United States and sold the majority of their final output in the domestic market. Space prohibits documentation of these assumptions; however, they rest upon data contained in ibid., Cherington, "Some Aspects of the Wool Trade," and U.S. Tariff Board, *Wool and Manufactures of Wool* (Washington, D.C., 1912).

sponsor sheepshearing exhibitions at county fairs. The National Wool Growers Association, formed in 1865, might have provided the nucleus of a central marketing agency, but during the early years of its existence the Association expended most of its energy and funds lobbying in Congress for increases in the tariff on imported wool.[56]

56. Harry James Brown, "The Fleece and the Loom: Wool Growers and Wool Manufacturers during the Civil War," *Business History Review* 29 (March 1955): 1–27, discusses the formation of the National Wool Growers Association.

CHAPTER IV

Quests for Wool and Workers

In the normal course of their search for raw material, the small woolen mills of the Middle West became important agents and buyers in the region's wool market. The brokers and commission houses, organized to collect and ship raw wool to the textile factories of the East, served midwestern mills by allowing them to reduce fleece inventories, thus freeing capital for other purposes. In 1870 the woolen mill at Morenci, Michigan, consistently placed an order at least once a month with the woolhouse of Thomas McGraw at Detroit.[1] By dealing with several wool merchants, mills could compare prices, and the existence of many such firms assured manufacturers of locating the correct quantities and types of wool. Throughout the 1870s, the Watkins Mill purchased fleece from at least eight different Missouri dealers in Cameron, Kansas City, St. Joseph, and St. Louis, and from concerns in Chicago and Philadelphia. Commission merchants dispatched small samples of wool to mills, and, following a close inspection and a shrinkage test, the two firms frequently haggled until both parties could agree on price.

Woolhouses also assisted mills by extending credit on purchases. Commission merchants usually gave a liberal grace period on sales, with allowance of additional time by acceptance of a promissory note, but the interest charge for such service was normally high and varied widely among dealers. Such wool merchants as Benjamin McLean of Kansas City, and Coates Brothers in Philadelphia, usually received 10 percent interest on accounts carried beyond two months, but this by no means represented a standard rate.[2] In 1871, Thomas McGraw of Detroit imposed an additional 8 percent charge on the Constantine Mills of Constantine, Michigan, for its unpaid balance which had been delinquent for only thrity days.[3] On one sale of 20,000 pounds of fleece in November 1864, Nevins and Company of Boston agreed to accept cash payment in forty days, yet collected interest after the fifteenth day.[4] Most midwestern mills took full advantage of the credit extended by woolhouses but violently objected to the high rates charged on overdue accounts.

Manufacturers also utilized the services of commission men in order to market the surplus fleece which they acquired through direct purchases at the factory. Faced with slow and sometimes unreliable transportation, many farmers sold clips in their immediate neighborhoods rather than risk an eastern shipment to an unpredictable market. In years when sheep raisers produced large quantities, mills collected wool inventories by bartering finished cloth and yarn for wool, or by direct cash payments. Excess lots, or wool types not suited to local fabrication, were normally consigned to commission houses for disposal in other markets. Such was the case when the woolen factory at Northville, Michigan, shipped large quantities of fleece to several different wool dealers in 1864 and again in 1865.[5] Although purchases of local wool exceeded plant capacity in some years, such buying encouraged farmers to trade at the mill, and many factory owners deemed it good business.

Cloth producers could receive cash advances from commis-

1. Morenci Woolen Mills to Thomas McGraw, Morenci, Michigan, October 20, November 16, and December 20, 1870, in the Thomas McGraw Papers, Burton Historical Collection, Detroit Public Library, Detroit.

2. Invoices, Benjamin McLean and Company, Kansas City, March 22, 1879, and Coates Brothers, Philadelphia, February 27, 1890, to the Watkins Mill, in the Watkins Mill Collection, Jackson County, Missouri, Historical Society Archives, Independence.

3. Constantine Woolen Mills to McGraw, Constantine, Michigan, September 25, 1871, McGraw Papers.

4. Nevins and Company to McGraw, Boston, November 3, 1864, McGraw Papers.

5. Wool Book, 1864–1866, Northville Woolen Mills, in the Michigan Historical Collections, University of Michigan, Ann Arbor.

sion merchants on shipments of raw wool consigned to them, thus relieving the drain on the manufacturer's capital, but most wool dealers exacted an interest charge on such money. Given a good market, mills might show a small profit from fleece sales even after woolhouses deducted as much as 6 percent for handling, insurance, selling, sorting, and storage. Wool speculation, however, sometimes proved to be a dangerous venture. For example, the North Star Woolen Mills of Minneapolis sustained heavy losses on large quantities of local fleece purchased at inflated prices during 1874, and bankruptcy eventually resulted.[6]

While buying on their own account, some mills earned extra money by purchasing for woolhouses in larger cities. In the 1860s and early 1870s, for example, woolen factories at Vassar and Ypsilanti, Michigan, and at Mishawaka and South Bend, Indiana, collected commissions as the agents of Thomas McGraw at Detroit. Although manufacturers did not openly express dissatisfaction at the practice, most wool dealers functioned as both buyers and sellers. That is, such firms purchased fleece on orders for local mills, and at the same time sold extra lots received from these factories.[7]

To avoid the charges of woolhouses and to encourage farmers to sell clips locally, some midwestern mills employed commission merchants only when necessity dictated their use. And, since many agent buyers proved incapable of accurately grading raw wool, this further prompted manufacturers to deal directly with sheep raisers. For example, by the summer of 1873, the Island Woolen Mills of Baraboo, Wisconsin, had "abandoned the buying of wool through agents for the reason that so many lots [were] bought without proper discrimination

6. Copy of "An Interview, Lucile Kane with William G. Northup, in the Minneapolis Offices of the North Star Woolen Mills," November 16, 1949, in the Minnesota Historical Society, St. Paul.

7. Both custom and law frowned upon this practice in buying and selling cotton in the South. See Harold D. Woodman, "Itinerant Cotton Merchants of the Antebellum South," *Agricultural History* 40 (April 1966): 88.

as regards quality and condition."[8] Island's owners urged Wisconsin farmers to ship fleece to the factory in Baraboo, receive a price equal to the market in Chicago or Milwaukee, and save the selling commission.[9] Few mills, however, found it possible to rely on local woolgrowers, and as the sheep population of the Middle West declined after 1890, most factories came to depend almost entirely on commission houses to supply them with raw material. Even the Island Mills had returned to the use of wool dealers and agents by the turn of the century.

As midwestern wool production increased, fleece became an important item in the general produce trade of smalltown merchants. The concurrent development of residentiary woolen mills provided area storekeepers with a convenient market for the increasing quantities of raw wool received from customers. Therefore, a close working relationship quickly developed between rural stores and the local woolen factory. Almost from their opening, mills received wool from merchants within an approximate fifty-mile radius of the plant. As late as 1902, the Carrollton Woolen Mill, at Carrollton, Missouri, procured fleece from storekeepers in the Missouri towns of Bogard, Browning, Gallatin, Milan, Purden, Richmond, and Samples.[10] Merchants made direct purchases of wool for factories, solicited information on the quantity and quality of fleece held by local farmers, and stored wool in anticipation of mill needs.

In addition to buying from woolgrowers directly at the plant, from rural storekeepers, and from commission merchants, many midwestern factories obtained raw material by dispatching their own buyers to local farms during the shearing season. The lack of uniformity among clips and the dishonesty of a few farmers encouraged the use of mill buyers, since they could carefully examine entire lots and estimate overall shrinkage and quality, rather than depending upon a small sample. The

8. Island Woolen Mills to A. H. Williard, Baraboo, Wisconsin, June 4, 1873, in the Island Woolen Mills Collection, State Historical Society of Wisconsin, Madison.

9. Ibid.

10. William McIntyre to Watkins Mill, Carrollton, Missouri, June 16, 1902, Watkins Collection.

ideal mill buyer possessed experience in cloth fabrication because a miscalculation in shrinkage of more than 1 or 2 percent might mean the difference between profit and loss for a factory operating on a close margin. Therefore, such agents were often part owners of a mill or closely connected with production.

The method of direct buying employed by the Watkins Mill typified the approach of several other midwestern factories. The firm's agent, Herman Belt, toured farms in northwest Missouri during the 1870s to collect small lots of wool in his own wagon or to conclude agreements with woolgrowers to deliver fleece to the factory. In payment, Belt issued promissory notes which instructed the Watkins Mill to pay the bearer cash on demand. By 1879, Judson Watkins, part owner of the firm, had assumed the direct-buying duties and made annual visits to area shearing pens during the spring and summer. In one brief trip in 1884, Watkins wrote checks in payment for over 25,000 pounds of wool purchased within forty miles of the plant.[11] Through face-to-face contacts with farmers, he could usually determine woolgrower attitudes. Watkins adjusted his buying procedure to fit the particular situation, and, as indicated by a letter to his brother in 1879, he occasionally played the waiting game: "I stayed in Smithville [Missouri] last night. . . . They are waiting for better offers. I will have no trouble to buy next week and I think they will be tired of waiting. . . . I think I can make more money by staying in the neighborhood, posting myself as to where the wool is and by salting the farmers."[12]

Even when purchased by a mill, wool clipped in the Middle West sometimes passed through the hands of several people and firms before its sale to a factory within the region. During July and August 1908, the woolen mill at South Bend, Indiana, bought approximately 100,000 pounds of fleece from local farmers. In turn, South Bend stored its purchase with Weil and Company, Fort Wayne commission merchants. South Bend instructed Weil in May 1909 to release the wool to Swift and

11. Judson Watkins to John Watkins, Linkville, Missouri, June 15, 1884, in the private collection of Mrs. Manfred Weber, Shawnee Mission, Kansas.
12. Ibid., May 15, 1879, Watkins Collection.

Company, who then contacted the Flint Woolen Mills of Flint, Michigan. After much haggling over quality and price, Flint's owners finally agreed to buy at least 30,000 pounds of the lot.[13]

Midwestern farmers realized that domestic supplies of wool sometimes failed to meet industry demands, and during such periods they attempted to play one buyer against another in an effort to receive higher prices. In those years when clips were especially light, midwestern factories faced increased competition for raw material from wool dealers within the region and from the buying agents of commission merchants and textiles mills in the East. By 1870, Vassar Woolen Mills of Vassar, Michigan, found local farmers reluctant to sell because Boston agents swarmed over the Detroit area offering high prices,[14] and an owner of the Watkins Mill blamed Missouri's "fool country buyers who are trying to spring the market" for his inability to purchase fleece in 1881.[15] As late as 1909, Flint Woolen Mills in Michigan felt surrounded by eastern commission men who had entered "every town of any size in the state."[16]

The general level of agricultural prosperity also affected the wool trade. The high wheat prices of the late 1860s permitted some farmers the luxury of holding fleece for several months awaiting higher quotations. For example, William Hinsdell, a wool buyer in Grand Rapids, Michigan, complained to Thomas McGraw that the advancing price of grain in 1866 had caused sheep raisers in that part of the state to store their wool until the market improved.[17] Confronted with a similar problem in

13. Flint Woolen Mills, Flint, Michigan, to J. H. Howard and Son, May 7, 1909, and H. T. Thompson and Company, May 15, 1909, in the Stone-Atwood Company Records, Michigan Historical Collections, University of Michigan, Ann Arbor. Stone-Atwood Company became the Flint Woolen Mills around 1900, but to avoid confusion all future reference citations will be Stone-Atwood Collection.

14. Vassar Woolen Mills to McGraw, Vassar, Michigan, July 1, 1870, McGraw Papers.

15. John Watkins to A. J. Watkins, Gower, Missouri, June 10, 1881, Watkins Collection.

16. Flint Woolen Mills to M. J. Smiley, Flint, Michigan, April 26, 1909, Stone-Atwood Collection.

17. William Hinsdell to McGraw, Grand Rapids, Michigan, August 31, 1866, McGraw Papers.

1873, the Island Woolen Mills advised its buyer to wait out the farmers until they realized that they were being offered a fair price, and then to "carry a copy of any Chicago daily paper and let them see for themselves what it is bringing."[18]

Although manufacturers in the Middle West occasionally bemoaned the scarcity of fleece, or complained of its high price, they usually found wools of suitable quality and in sufficient quantities within the region. The 1878 fleece purchases of the North Star Woolen Mills of Minneapolis, for example, amounted to 814,209 pounds, over 71 percent of which they bought in Iowa, Minnesota, and Wisconsin.[19] And, although the region's farmers had already started to abandon woolgrowing by the early 1890s, Appleton Mills in Wisconsin continued to find the major portion of its raw material within two hundred miles of the factory.

The costs of transporting raw wool from the Middle West to the eastern textile industry, coupled with the expense of shipping finished cloth from the East to the midwestern market, afforded woolen mills of the region protection from competitive fabrics of equal quality. For example, one pound of fleece, costing approximately twenty cents, was required to manufacture one yard of cassimere similar to the type produced by most pioneer woolen factories in the 1870s. Although the wool in a yard of such material accounted for nearly one-half the manufacturing costs, it could be moved by rail from the St. Louis market to the Atlantic coast for one cent.[20] On the return trip, woolen textiles shipped from New York to most small towns in the Midwest during the same time period paid freight charges of nearly two cents per pound.[21] Because they were not subject

18. Island Woolen Mills to A. B. Darling, Baraboo, Wisconsin, June 24, 1873, Island Collection.
19. Wool Book, 1877–1881, in the North Star Woolen Mill Company Records, Minnesota Historical Society, St. Paul.
20. The cost calculation on cassimere is from the Watkins Collection.
21. For example, freight charges on dry goods shipped from New York to Appleton, Wisconsin, in 1874 amounted to 1.9 cents per pound. Chicago and North Western Railroad to William Robertson,

to these transportation costs, midwestern mills enjoyed an initial advantage of approximately three cents per pound over factories in the East on the sale of cassimere in the midwestern market.

The expenses incurred in the transportation of wool and the finished product, in manufacturing, and in buying raw wool and selling finished cloth comprised the total costs of all woolen mills.[22] For purposes of analysis, it is assumed that both the buying and selling costs of factories in the East and Middle West were equal,[23] but because of greater efficiency and economies of scale, the manufacturing costs of eastern mills were less than those of most midwestern factories. And, presumably, the manufacturing cost advantages of mills in the East were less than their total transport expenses.[24] Therefore, the costs of transportation constituted the key factor which protected residentiary woolen mills in the Middle West from outside competition. Eastern firms could not sell coarse- and medium-quality fabrics in the midwestern market unless they priced below their

---

Chicago, August 1, 1874, in the Appleton Mills Collection, State Historical Society of Wisconsin, Madison. Freight rates on eastern goods can also be found in H. T. Newcomb, *Changes in the Rate of Charge for Railroads and Other Transportation Services*, United States Department of Agriculture, Div. of Stat., Misc. ser., *Bulletin 15*.

22. To simplify the discussion, the comparative costs of servicing the equity and debt of eastern and midwestern mills are assumed to be equal and, therefore, ignored. Lower interest rates in the East perhaps provided factories in that region with cost advantages in servicing the debt. However, most woolen mills in the Midwest were family-dominated partnerships and corporations with a small capitalization, and at times this no doubt tended to reduce the dividend drain.

23. If either party enjoyed cost advantages in buying and selling, mills in the Middle West definitely held the upper hand because of their close proximity to raw wool supplies and the market for cheap textiles.

24. The lower limit of the difference between the costs of an eastern and midwestern mill was set by the sum of the transport costs on raw wool and the finished product. Although the nature of the material available prohibits an exact calculation, the sum of the total transportation expenses and the manufacturing cost advantages constituted the upper limit of the cost differences between factories in the East and Middle West.

manufacturing costs.[25] To put it another way, mills in the East obviously failed to obtain manufacturing cost advantages large enough to overcome the transportation differential.

The types of cloth fabricated by nearly all midwestern woolen mills did not require hiring elaborately trained laborers for all operations. Factory owners found it necessary to offer relatively high wages in order to attract competent dyers, finishers, and weavers, but the remaining steps in production could often be assigned to unskilled workers. Since yarn constituted an important retail line for most manufacturers, employment of women and children to tend spindles proved a profitable venture. As early as 1850, a woolen mill at St. Louis engaged 15 men and 10 women, and the November 1894 payroll of the Flint Woolen Mills in Michigan included 24 females among the firm's 58 employees. In its 1903–1904 report, the Minnesota Bureau of Labor listed 110 men, 100 women, and 6 children at North Star in Minneapolis.[26]

Typical of the times, women toiled alongside men in most woolen mill departments, yet suffered wage discrimination for the same type of work. The forty cent difference between the daily wages of men and women who labored in the North Star finishing room in 1874 corresponded closely to the differences in pay in a Massachusetts textile factory during the same year.[27] Men also enjoyed preferential treatment during those periods when plants failed to operate at full capacity. In March 1891, Appleton Mills, for example, sought weavers for the coming season, yet made it perfectly clear that women employed for

25. Of course, total costs plus the markup determined the prices charged by manufacturers selling in the midwestern market, and the amount of the markup was a function of the costs.

26. *Hunt's Merchants' Magazine and Commercial Review* 24 (March 1851): 316; Time Book, Flint Woolen Mills, June 1893– September 1896, Stone-Atwood Collection; *Ninth Biennial Report of the Bureau of Labor of the State of Minnesota, 1903–1904* (Minneapolis, Minn., 1904), 100.

27. Workman's Time Book, 1874–1879, North Star Records; *Fifteenth Annual Report of the Commissioner of Labor, 1900: A Compilation of Wages in Commercial Countries from Official Sources* (Washington, D.C., 1900), 1: 565.

such work would be forced to give up their positions to men when production fell off in the fall.[28]

Like the farmer and many others in the West, laborers in midwestern woolen mills seemed perpetually dissatisfied with their lot and constantly searched for new positions. A stream of job inquiries poured into woolen company offices throughout the 1860s and 1870s, and letters from such people indicated that to alleviate their feelings of discontent, many had moved from one plant to another hoping to find steady employment and better pay. For example, a carder in Carthage, Missouri, in 1884 had worked at a large Philadelphia factory and at smaller concerns in Ohio, while in 1895, W. H. Kelley, a weaver, offered the Watkins Mill recommendations from factories in Appleton and Neenah, Wisconsin, in addition to references from other pioneer woolen mills.[29]

Broken machines, business recessions, fires, inadequate water for steam engines, and inclement weather all added to unstable employment in the woolen mills of the Midwest. Small factories failed to run steadily, and laborers suffered when plant machinery stood idle. Many mills produced cloth only nine months each year, and, typical of such firms, the Horton Woolen Mill in Roanoke, Indiana, did not start its machinery until early March of 1868, following a winter shutdown of several months. During 1900, woolen factories at Baraboo, Wisconsin; Fairfield, Iowa; Faribault, Minnesota; Hanover, Illinois; and St. Joseph, Missouri, were stopped from a few days to several weeks by heavy rains, damaged equipment, or slack orders.[30] The local and national level of economic prosperity also affected job opportunities. When the woolen mill at Springfield, Illinois, reduced its work force in 1878, its employees

28. Appleton Mills to C. C. Hill, Appleton, Wisconsin, March 28, 1891, Appleton Collection.

29. George Fisher, Carthage, Missouri, April 2, 1884, and W. H. Kelley, Westvale, Massachusetts, October 27, 1895, to John Watkins, Watkins Collection.

30. Woolen Manufacturers' Association of the Northwest, *First Annual Report* (Chicago, 1868), 26; *Fibre and Fabric* 31 (February 17, 1900): 6, (May 26, 1900): 176, and (July 28, 1900): 288; *Textile World* 18 (February 1900): 309, and 19 (November 1900): 862.

initiated a search of other states for positions. And, although the owners of the Flint Woolen Mills prided themselves for running more steadily than any other factory in Michigan, they ceased operation for six months in 1908 because of a financial panic.[31]

In addition to periodic unemployment, workers repeatedly voiced dissatisfaction with the wages offered by midwestern mills, and thus the region's factory owners encountered difficulty in attracting laborers. For example, in refusing a job offer at the Watkins Mill in 1884, Edward Leibard, a dyer in Richmond, Indiana, chided the Watkins manager on the proposed remuneration, suggesting that his firm could not expect to attract competent talent with such a low pay schedule.[32] Hutchinson and Company, of Appleton, Wisconsin, received numerous letters during the 1870s from mill operatives in eastern states arguing that the wages offered by that concern would not justify a move west.[33]

Complaints of eastern workers wishing to move west continued and pointed up the fact that although money wages in midwestern woolen factories increased steadily from 1860 to 1900, such advances merely kept pace with textile mill wages on the national level. The pay of employees at Appleton, Faribault, Flint, North Star, and Watkins corresponded closely to the wages received by operatives in Connecticut, Maine, Massachusetts, New Hampshire, and New Jersey during similar time periods.[34]

31. Flint Woolen Mills to Nora Bird, Flint, Michigan, April 28, 1909, Stone-Atwood Collection.

32. Edward Leibard to John Watkins, Richmond, Indiana, April 21, 1884, Watkins Collection.

33. For examples, see folder marked "Letters of Application," in the Appleton Collection.

34. Wages at these five midwestern mills were taken from company records and correspondence, and compared to wages listed in *Report of the Commissioner of Labor, 1900*, 1: 245, 565–67; U.S., Congress, Senate, *Wholesale Prices, Wages, and Transportation*, 52d Cong., 2d sess., Senate Report 1394, part 4, 1463–1560; Julius Forstman, *The Wool Manufacture in America and Europe* (Boston, 1911), 33–35; U.S. Department of Labor, Bureau of Statistics, *Bulletin 128* (1913), *Bulletin 150* (1914), and *Bulletin 238* (1915).

Nationally, real wages showed marked advances, as the purchasing power of the dollar climbed following the panic of 1873. However, many factories, especially those in isolated areas, provided workers with extra benefits, and this prohibits a comparison of real wages between eastern and midwestern laborers. One can only surmise that mill employees in the Midwest enjoyed similar increases in real wages during these years. In addition, some woolen factories, such as Faribault in Minnesota, La Porte in Indiana, and Watkins in Missouri, offered workers company-owned cottages, and a few employees received extra compensation in the form of farm produce. For example, some wage earners at the Eagle Mills near Indianapolis in the 1870s were allotted a cow, chickens, and a garden plot without cost.[35]

Employed laborers in midwestern mills frequently contacted other factory owners within the region seeking jobs which offered increases in pay and steadier employment. Yet, by the turn of the century, wages in the woolen industry throughout the eight states of the region tended to be equal. The author has examined correspondence among millowners, restricted from direct citation by its holder, which helps in part to account for the similarity of pay scales offered to textile workers. Around 1900 several manufacturers entertained the possibility of establishing standard wage rates in the major woolen mills in Illinois, Iowa, Indiana, Michigan, Missouri, and Wisconsin. A few woolen producers, however, rejected the proposal, arguing that each locality possessed unique problems and circumstances which would limit the effectiveness of such a plan. Although factory owners apparently failed to adopt a formal wage-fixing policy, mills frequently exchanged information on employees and wages, and most plant managers knew the prevailing pay schedules of other factories in the region.

Millowners cooperated in other ways. Several of the major factories of the region collaborated to prevent the hiring of troublesome employees, and the labor blacklist, feared by some

35. *Indianapolis Sunday Star*, August 27, 1911.

eastern workers, had its counterpart in the Midwest. Most manufacturers felt that it was legally too risky to sign a formal agreement pledging themselves to refrain from hiring certain workers, but factories which experienced labor problems circumvented the legality of the situation by mailing lists of unacceptable employees to other concerns in the region requesting their moral support. And, both millowners and managers appear to have understood the implied definition of morality in such cases.[36]

Typical of the American business community during the nineteenth century, wool manufacturers in the Middle West usually refused to negotiate with their workers in any manner which suggested collective bargaining. In April 1910, when the South Bend, Indiana, Woolen Mill faced a strike of its weavers following union organization, the management immediately ceased production, closed the plant, and sought to hire new workers.[37] And, in Michigan, with the walkout of the Yale Woolen Mill weavers in the spring of 1910, Yale's owners made no effort to ascertain if they were justified, but took the position that "if they had any grievance . . . they should have notified us in a proper manner, instead of stopping their looms"[38] Most of the region's wool manufacturers appeared quite willing to discuss employee complaints, including low wages, but strictly on an individual basis.

As early as the 1890s, midwestern woolen factories had difficulty in locating skilled personnel. Since good weavers could normally do well in any pursuit requiring good eyesight and rapid hand movements, retaining their services became difficult as industrial development continued in the region. Several mills suffered from a shortage of qualified weavers, and, as only one illustration, in November 1890, Appleton Mills appealed to Wis-

36. The author has read extensive correspondence which indicates that millowners in the Midwest cooperated closely in the hiring of new employees.
37. Sands Hart to F. J. Harwood, Racine, Wisconsin, April 20, 1910, Appleton Collection.
38. Edward Audreae to F. J. Harwood, Yale, Michigan, April 23, 1910, Appleton Collection.

consin factories in Baraboo, Beaver Dam, Cedarburg, Janesville, Racine, Reedsburg, and Sheboygan Falls, pleading for their help in filling weaving vacancies.[39] Seasoned carders, dyers, finishers, and loom-fixers also became scarce. The owners of woolen mills at Flint, Michigan, and Duluth, Minnesota, to mention only two cases, complained of their inability to acquire competent finishers in 1909.[40]

Millowners in the Middle West employed various methods in an effort to attract laborers, and when they failed to find workers locally, most manufacturers searched in the East. For example, in June and July 1900, woolen mills at Baraboo, Wisconsin; Clinton, Michigan; and Rochester, Minnesota, ran advertisements in Wade's *Fibre and Fabric,* a Boston publication.[41] During the 1870s, the Watkins Mill utilized the classified section of *The Woolen Mill News,*[42] sought employees through local newspapers, and maintained a close correspondence with those factories in the region that exchanged information on available workers. In its quest for loom-fixers and weavers in July 1900, Flint Woolen Mills contacted manufacturers in several states, while advertising in a New York trade magazine, *The Textile Manufacturers' Journal;* when such efforts produced no results, Flint's managers then attempted to raid other midwestern mills by trying to lure employed workers from their jobs.[43]

Locating skilled labor constituted a problem for most woolen mills from their first day of operation, and as early as 1868 several manufacturers in the Midwest proposed that factory

39. See letters from Appleton Mills to these firms dated November 24, 1890, in the Appleton Collection.

40. Flint Woolen Mills to John Belcher, Flint, Michigan, December 8, 1909, Stone-Atwood Collection.

41. *Fibre and Fabric* 31 (June 23, 1900): 2; (July 14, 1900): 3; and (July 21, 1900): 3.

42. William H. Dillingham, a Louisville, Kentucky, textile-machinery dealer, printed and circulated *The Woolen Mill News* in the 1870s. Circulation included the South and the states of Illinois, Indiana, Iowa, Missouri, and Ohio.

43. Flint Woolen Mills, Flint, Michigan, to R. R. Street and Company, *Textile Manufacturers' Journal,* July 5, 1900, and Fred Howard and James Hallett, July 6, 1900, Stone-Atwood Collection.

owners aid one another in their efforts to find personnel. As labor shortages became acute in the region's woolen industry, mills continued to favor close cooperation in searching for workers and also desired a gentleman's agreement to prohibit raiding. Attempts to entice laborers to leave a local plant often produced an immediate reaction from the offended millowner. In 1910, when the Beaver Dam Woolen Mill in southeastern Wisconsin advertised for workers in a Reedsburg, Wisconsin, newspaper, officials of the Reedsburg Woolen Mill were quick to respond to the threat. In a letter to Beaver Dam officers, F. J. Harwood, a Reedsburg executive, reprimanded the factory manager, arguing that cooperation, not competition, should characterize relations between two neighboring firms. Harwood concluded his letter with a friendly request: "We are 'up against' the same proposition in the matter of help you are and . . . to take a weaver away from us is to weaken us that much. It may be alright from a competitors stand-point but not a helpful one, so thought we would come to you direct and ask you not to try and get our help away from us."[44]

Since midwestern woolen concerns seemingly felt unable to offer premium wages, salary schedules proved an inadequate drawing card in their quest for workers.[45] Therefore, some manufacturers included other inducements designed to aid in the solicitation of new laborers and the retention of current employees. Plants in rural areas often constructed cottages to provide inexpensive housing for prospective operatives and their families, and thus argued that living expenses in their area were nominal. In general, the rental charges for company-owned dwellings did remain moderate, and in a few cases cheap

44. F. J. Harwood to Beaver Dam Woolen Mills, Appleton, Wisconsin, April 21, 1910, Appleton Collection. Appleton Mills also owned a woolen factory at Reedsburg, Wisconsin.

45. One might debate the point that had midwestern millowners offered higher wages than those prevailing in the East they would have been able to attract workers. As W. R. Maclaurin and Charles A. Meyers have shown, wages may not provide a major incentive to relocate. See "Wages and the Movement of Factory Labor," *Quarterly Journal of Economics* 57 (February 1943): 241–64.

housing was an effective recruiting device. In an effort to obtain good employees and to discourage others from leaving, some eastern firms such as the Peace Dale Woolen Mill in Rhode Island, and the Talbot Mills of Billerica, Massachusetts, instituted profit-sharing and pension plans for their workers,[46] and a few factories in the Midwest followed suit. Appleton Mills laborers, for example, received an annual salary dividend of 4 percent beginning in January 1900.[47] And, F. J. Harwood, the Appleton president, received several inquiries from other firms who exhibited interest in the plan and desired to institute such a program in their respective factories. Mills in the Midwest which continued to search the eastern labor market for skilled workers usually found it necessary to provide prospective employees and their dependents with funds for travel and relocation. For example, in order to attract a weaver from Watertown, Massachusetts, in 1909, the Flint Woolen Mills were required to advance him the expense money for the journey west.[48]

The concept of the American West as a safety valve for discontented eastern laborers has invoked considerable interest among historians. As Fred Shannon has shown, few workers in Atlantic coast urban areas could accumulate the necessary expense money to migrate.[49] However, interpretations such as Shannon's draw too narrow a definition of the safety valve and overlook the broader influences of the West on eastern workers. Responses from some laborers in the East, indicating a willingness to move, and attempts by eastern factories to encourage workers to remain at their jobs, point up the real impact of the American West on eastern labor. Although few workers actually moved West, the very threat of doing so no doubt increased

46. Peter Stewart, "A Profit-Sharing System for the Peace Dale Mill in Rhode Island," *Textile History Review* 4 (July 1963): 129–32; *Textile World Record* 25 (April 1903): 81.

47. F. J. Harwood to Scranton Stove Works, Appleton, Wisconsin, February 2, 1900, Appleton Collection. A few years later Appleton also established an accident insurance fund for its employees.

48. Flint Woolen Mills to W. J. Benjamin, Flint, Michigan, November 4, 13, and 22, 1909, Stone-Atwood Collection.

49. Fred A. Shannon, "A Post Mortem on the Labor-Safety-Valve Theory," *Agricultural History* 19 (January 1945): 31–37.

wages in the eastern job market, while making laborers in the East less radical. In this broader sense the safety valve did exist.

Mills occasionally lured an eastern worker away from his job, but after 1900 most wool manufacturers in the Middle West gave up in disgust. By 1908, the Flint Woolen Mills had abandoned the search for employees in the East, since good men could "get more pay in a better position than it is possible to get in the West,"[50] and four years later the president of the woolen factory at Clinton, Michigan, concluded that those laborers who could be persuaded to leave an eastern mill were not desirable workers.[51] In July 1912, the manager of the Island Woolen Mills in Baraboo, Wisconsin, advised other manufacturers in the region that since the factories of the Midwest were scattered and individually isolated, the only solution to the labor problem was to disregard the eastern market and to develop a complement of local operatives so content with their positions they would not wish to move.[52]

Some wool manufacturers paid their workers with money and goods and services. For the hours spent at spinning and weaving in the Murray Woolen Mill in Indiana around 1850, David Tiffany received cash, cloth, credit at a local store, groceries, and room and board.[53] Watkins Mill employees sometimes took part of their pay in food, dry goods, and hardware from the company store housed in one small room of the factory. Payment in farm produce or stock from the store allowed millowners to shift part of their capital burden for wages onto eastern mercantile houses for several months since they provided store supplies on credit.

Laborers in most midwestern woolen plants toiled long hours,

50. Flint Woolen Mills to the Joseph M. Wade Publishing Company, Flint, Michigan, April 5, 1908, Stone-Atwood Collection.

51. W. S. Kimball to F. J. Harwood, Clinton, Michigan, July 18, 1912, Appleton Collection.

52. Island Woolen Mills to F. J. Harwood, Baraboo, Wisconsin, July 18, 1912, Appleton Collection.

53. Account Book, William Murray Woolen Mill, Wayne County, Indiana, 1847–1854, William Murray Account Books, in the Indiana Historical Society, Indianapolis.

even though factory running-time corresponded closely to that of eastern firms in the same industry. Until 1892, male weavers in Massachusetts woolen mills labored sixty hours per week and the six, ten-hour days worked by Faribault factory employees in the late 1800s typified the production time of other concerns in the region.[54] Increased orders occasionally encouraged factories to expand operating hours. The Warrensburg Woolen Mill in Missouri periodically ran at night, and heavy cloth orders necessitated a night shift at Appleton in 1891 and a seventy-two-hour workweek at the Faribault mill in 1892.[55]

Information concerning actual working conditions in mid-western woolen mills is fragmentary. The author has uncovered no diaries or personal accounts which might indicate labor attitudes toward management, monotony of duties, restrictions and regulations, and sanitary conditions. As a general rule, all millowners demanded steady, industrious, and sober employees, who paid their debts. In isolated rural communities manufacturers could more carefully observe and regulate the personal lives of their workers. By providing company-owned houses, woolen producers encouraged entire families to work in the mill, thereby helping to alleviate labor shortages, and they could also more readily maintain surveillance over them. Married workers with families at the Eagle Mills near Indianapolis around 1880, for example, were required to live in nearby cottages, while unmarried males took rooms in the factory owner's large house.[56] Such an arrangement might prove highly restrictive, but, on the other hand, in some cases it perhaps generated a warm personal relationship between the employer and his workers.

Since wool manufacturers in the Midwest failed to mention a lack of unskilled workers, one can only assume that they faced

54. Frank H. Klemer, "The History of the Faribault Woolen Mills" (paper read before the Rice County, Minnesota, Historical Society, October 22, 1940, copy in the Minnesota Historical Society, St. Paul).

55. Ibid.; Appleton Mills to James Chambers, Appleton, Wisconsin, April 23, 1891, Appleton Collection.

56. *Indianapolis Sunday Star,* October 26, 1930; *Indianapolis Star,* August 9, 1942.

no shortage of such labor. However, the location and employment of individuals with special skills in textile production
proved to be a constant source of irritation throughout the
period from 1860 to 1920. Prior to 1890, workers in midwestern
factories were unhappy with the low pay and periodic layoffs,
but most mills failed to correct these two complaints that
seemed to hinder the acquisition and retention of reliable, qualified employees. Moreover, wages and fringe benefits in the
Middle West were generally not sufficient to attract workers
from the East. After 1890, the shortage of skilled labor became
even more critical and is an indication that midwestern woolen
mills were not paying wages competitive with those offered by
other industries in the region, or, that for several years, young
workers who might have been trained had stopped entering the
textile labor force.

The woolen factories of the Middle West obviously were not
labor-oriented. Since the New England and Middle Atlantic
states contained large numbers of textile firms which provided
a pool of trained employees, an eastern cloth producer possessed a decided advantage in acquiring competent personnel.
The problems encountered in obtaining skilled labor, however,
were compensated by the advantages and convenience of manufacturing close to the market. An analysis of production for,
and service to, that local market constitutes a significant chapter in the economic history of the Midwest.

CHAPTER V

Production and Sales
in the Local and Regional Market

The midwestern internal market developed rapidly after the Civil War, and by the early 1870s wool manufacturers of the region found it unnecessary to order minor mill supplies from firms located along the Atlantic seaboard. The Watkins Mill in Missouri, for example, purchased chemicals and dye stuffs from Chicago and St. Louis, cotton bagging for woolsacks from Kansas City, and belting used to drive power equipment from St. Joseph. Further north in Michigan, the Stone-Atwood Company found these and other items readily available in Chicago, Detroit, St. Louis, and Fort Wayne, Indiana.

Although frequently used supplies proved locally abundant, textile machine builders were not. A few eastern machinery manufacturers dispatched their own salesmen to the Midwest to solicit business, but most preferred to depend upon independent dealers who established small showrooms in the larger cities of the region. In addition to offering a line of mill equipment such dealers often combined machinery sales with other activities closely connected to wool manufacturing. For example, in the 1870s, J. B. Carson Brothers, St. Louis dry goods commission merchants, took machinery orders for the Bridesburg Manufacturing Company of Philadelphia and the C. G. Sargent Company of Graniteville, Massachusetts. Wool dealers such as J. P. Thompson in Milwaukee, and Merritt and Coughlen in Indianapolis also attempted to sell woolen textile appliances to millowners throughout the Middle West.[1]

A few businessmen concentrated all their efforts on the sale of mill machinery to pioneer manufacturers. For example, William H. Dillingham rented a large warehouse in Louisville, Kentucky, in November 1869 and then asked the C. G. Sargent Company and other machine builders in the East to send him textile equipment to display locally. He offered to set up such appliances for exhibit, to call on millowners in the West, and to take orders, all in return for a 10 percent selling commission.[2] Dillingham's proposal netted quick results, and by April 1871, in Indiana alone, he had sold Sargent machinery to woolen factories in Greensburg, Indianapolis, Jeffersonville, New Albany, and Richmond. Once a sale was made, Dillingham urged other wool manufacturers to visit mills where his line of machinery was in operation. This was the case when he sent an interested party to the woolen factory in Jeffersonville, Indiana, in July 1870, to inspect a recently installed burr picker.[3]

Dillingham also sought to reach new customers through the circulation of his own trade newspaper. During the early 1870s, he published *The Woolen Mill News* monthly and mailed it free to textile manufacturers and workers throughout most of the Middle West and South. In this paper he advertised his own line of machinery, ran articles and stories of interest to factory owners and their employees, and included a classified section listing eastern and western mills seeking labor, workers wishing to change positions, and secondhand equipment for sale or trade. Through editorials, Dillingham praised the merits of hometown manufacturing and heralded the advantages of western woolen mills over factories located in the East.[4]

1. Sales Circular, J. B. Carson Brothers, January 9, 1872, J. P. Thompson, Milwaukee, April 13, 1871, and Merritt and Coughlen, Indianapolis, January 25, 1867, to the C. G. Sargent Company, in the C. G. Sargent Collection, Merrimack Valley Textile Museum, North Andover, Massachusetts.

2. Albert O. Wilkes and William H. Dillingham to Sargent, Louisville, November 29 and December 11, 1869, Sargent Collection. Apparently Wilkes of Louisville joined Dillingham to establish the company, but Wilkes severed the partnership in November 1870.

3. Ibid., July 6, 1870, Sargent Collection.

4. For an example, see the August 1, 1875, copy of *The Woolen Mill News* in the Watkins Mill Collection, Jackson County, Missouri, Historical Society Archives, Independence.

In addition to employing their own salesmen and utilizing the services of independent dealers, textile machine builders often acted as agents for one another in the sale of noncompetitive equipment. Wool manufacturers constructing new plants desired many different types of mill machinery at one time, and if inquiries from the Midwest could be handled by one company, this expedited sales and shipment. Around 1870, the Bridesburg Manufacturing Company and Furbush and Gage, two woolen machine builders in Philadelphia, and the C. G. Sargent Company of Massachusetts accepted orders from midwestern customers for equipment produced by any one of the three firms. On such sales, the machine manufacturer receiving the order obtained the usual 10 percent commission.[5]

Machinery represented approximately 75 percent of the investment in most woolen factories, and freight charges on heavy, bulky appliances were high.[6] Therefore, since many manufacturers suffered from capital shortages, the costs of transportation in part influenced the size and type of machines in midwestern woolen mills. Since forests still existed in most areas of the region, woolen men quickly found that they could reduce transport expenses by constructing some equipment from wood, while ordering other necessary metal pieces from eastern concerns. For example, between 1867 and 1872, wool manufacturers in Albany, Missouri; Detroit and Vassar, Michigan; Minneapolis, Minnesota; Pittsfield, Illinois; and Seymour, Indiana, purchased only their fans and pulleys for wool dryers from a machine builder in the East, and fashioned frames and other apparatus locally. In the case of the Seymour Woolen Mill, the C. G. Sargent Company charged $150 for the fan and an additional $50 fee for the right to use it.[7] H. L. Weatherford of

5. Furbush and Gage to Sargent, Philadelphia, September 6, 1871, Sargent Collection.
6. As only one example, as late as 1893 freight charges on a wool dryer, costing $1,300, shipped from Graniteville, Massachusetts, to St. Joseph, Missouri, amounted to $105, and the machine manufacturer estimated that it would cost an additional $75 to send a mechanic to install the new appliance. C. G. Sargent Company to the Buell Manufacturing Company, Graniteville, December 15, 1893, Sargent Collection.

Unionville, Missouri, typified the requests of several others in the region when he asked an eastern firm in 1869 to make him a burring machine much smaller than those listed in their catalog, because it would "weigh less and not cost so much to get it delivered here."[8]

With homemade machines and equipment in other than standard sizes, it is not surprising that orders from midwestern woolen mills to eastern machine builders frequently contained crudely drawn sketches indicating that certain parts had to be placed in a unique position, or that the assembled appliance must fit into a specific space.[9] Factory owners depended upon machinery manufacturers to solve such engineering problems. Thus, Eastern firms attempting to sell textile machinery in the Middle West found that sales to the woolen mills of the region required an unusual amount of custom-order manufacturing.

High transportation costs, scarcity of capital, and protection from eastern competitors encouraged the widespread use of secondhand textile machinery in the Midwest. Millowners frequently purchased used cards, looms, and spinning machines from factories in the East, or within the region from plants which had suffered partial losses from fire. From the early 1880s until well after the turn of the century, the major textile trade journals listed secondhand machinery for sale by factories and mill equipment firms, and in time the volume of these appliances increased to such an extent that a few dealers could specialize in their purchase and sale.[10] In addition, manufac-

7. H. A. Scott to Sargent, Seymour, Indiana, August 20, 1867, Sargent Collection.

8. H. L. Weatherford to Sargent, Unionville, Missouri, November 14, 1869, Sargent Collection.

9. See Osceola Woolen Mill, Osceola, Iowa, January 9, 1871, Smith and Company, Philadelphia, July 25, 1868, and P. P. Eddy, Minneapolis, January 13, 1872, to Sargent, Sargent Collection.

10. Advertisements of W. S. Simmons, E. K. Watson, and the American Machinery Exchange, in *Fibre and Fabric* 13 (August 29, 1891): 3; 53 (September 3, 1910): 16; and 68 (August 14, 1920): 20. The rise of firms which specialized in the purchase and sale of used textile machinery indicated that most machine builders did not wish to accept trade-ins on new equipment, but preferred that millowners dispose of secondhand machinery.

turers wishing to dispose of used machines from established plants circulated sale notices. Thus, in woolen textiles the residentiary stage of manufacturing fostered the acquisition of secondhand equipment, and, from the standpoint of that industry, the pioneer experience invoked no revolutionary changes in machine technology. Indeed, isolation from the national market because of expensive inter- and intraregional transportation bred and nurtured obsolescence. In short, the residentiary stage of manufacturing modified technology to meet its own requirements rather than stimulating advances in that field.

Secondhand and sometimes obsolete woolen machinery continued to move westward as new mills opened in developing areas. Factories in the Middle West depended greatly on used equipment prior to 1890, and by 1900, machinery from those mills was being dismantled and moved to newly constructed plants in the Far West.[11] As long as pioneer manufacturers concentrated on production of cheap textiles that sold well in the local market, few saw need to buy up-to-date machinery if old equipment could still be repaired. Failure to adopt the latest technology offered no special dangers as long as factories in the Midwest remained protected from outside competition.

The distance from the Midwest to the Atlantic Coast, coupled with the fact that most pioneer woolen mills contained a conglomeration of homemade, new, and secondhand equipment, complicated the procurement of maintenance on machinery and the acquisition of replacement parts. A woolen factory in the East could usually obtain prompt service from mechanics sent out by machine builders, but a wool manufacturer located in an isolated midwestern community enjoyed no such luxury. Several millowners found it necessary to maintain a large stock

11. *Textile World* 19 (October 1900): 671; 20 (June 1901): 1151; 21 (September 1901): 547; 23 (December 1902): 1160; 24 (February 1903): 399; *Fibre and Fabric* 13 (March 28, 1891): 44. For a detailed discussion of the movement of textile machinery into the West consult Norman L. Crockett, "The Westward Movement and the Transit of American Machine Technology: The Case of Wool Manufacturing," *Nebraska Journal of Economics and Business* 8 (Summer 1969): 111–20.

of spare parts in order to avoid returning an entire machine to the manufacturer for repairs. Still, parts were often hard to find. When the woolen factory in Appleton, Wisconsin, needed a new drive chain for its washing machine in March 1891, the owners discovered that the washer manufacturer no longer sold machines of that model and had only one suggestion where the part might be found.[12] As late as 1909, Flint Woolen Mills suffered a serious delay in production while the company waited for an eastern machine shop to repair their damaged fulling mill.[13] Such cases pointed up disadvantages of an operation located hundreds of miles from eastern machinery suppliers. Spare-parts inventories tied up capital and broken equipment reduced factory running-time.

Woolen cloth for apparel constituted the major demand for the output of midwestern woolen mills prior to 1890. Before readymade clothing initiated a revolution in domestic consumption patterns, women of the region purchased cloth from local factories and storekeepers, and fashioned it into family garments. Farmers and residents of small towns seemed less affected by fashion than people congregated in large urban areas, and pioneer wool manufacturers concentrated men and machines on the production of coarse- and medium-grade fabrics offering warmth and durability rather than style. Although a few mills attempted product specialization, blankets, cassimeres, flannels, and jeans comprised the most important fabrics manufactured by woolen mills in the Middle West.[14]

Pioneer woolen factories utilized a heavy, coarse, and loosely

12. A. Hopkins and Company to Appleton Mills, Providence, March 31, 1891, in the Appleton Mills Collection, State Historical Society of Wisconsin, Madison.

13. Flint Woolen Mills to Republic Rubber Company, Flint, Michigan, November 15, 1909, in the Stone-Atwood Company Records, Michigan Historical Collections, University of Michigan, Ann Arbor.

14. Of the twenty-three Iowa woolen mills which reported product lines to the *Textile Manufacturers' Directory* in 1883, nineteen produced flannel, seventeen made blankets and cassimere, and eight manufactured jeans. A check of factories in other midwestern states indicated a similar proportion of mills fabricating these four items. *Textile Manufacturers' Directory* (New York, 1883), 59–61.

twisted yarn for blanket weaving. Although the resulting product might last for years, its scratchy surface often proved highly uncomfortable to human skin. Cassimere, a general term describing material normally employed in making men's clothing, could be woven plain or twilled, and constituted a medium-weight cloth of soft texture. The loosely woven, coarse-threaded flannel sold by nearly all woolen concerns in the region found extensive use as undergarments and bed coverings, and because it required little or no fulling and shearing, it could be produced cheaply and quickly. Jeans, or janes as they were often called, should not be confused with modern blue jeans or dungarees which are normally all cotton. The jean of the midwestern woolen mill consisted of a stout, twilled fabric used almost entirely for rough work clothing; the woolen homespun fabricated by pioneer women closely resembled factory-made jeans.[15]

The average midwestern woolen mill of 1870 constituted a small manufacturing unit. Two sets of cards, 5 looms, and 253 spindles composed its major machinery, and the annual consumption of 22,820 pounds of raw wool resulted in a yearly finished product valued at approximately $18,000. The number of employees varied seasonally, but on the average six men, three women, and one child labored nine to ten months each year in a steam- or water-powered plant which represented a total capital investment of $17,733.[16] Of course, no two factories were identical, but the Watkins Mill, which provided fabrics for a portion of northwest Missouri between 1861 and 1886, typified most firms of the region. Therefore, the Watkins method of converting raw wool into finished cloth and yarn offers a production model illustrative of pioneer wool manufacturing in general.[17]

15. The discussion of fabrics is based on *Cole's Encyclopedia of Dry Goods* (New York, 1900), 30, 91, 199, 280; Elizabeth Dyer, *Textile Fabrics* (Boston, 1927), 283, 294; Norma Hollen and Jane Saddler, *Textiles* (New York, 1955), 127; and William H. Dooley, *Textiles* (Boston, 1924), 153, 166.

16. Average midwestern mill in 1870 calculated from U.S. Department of Commerce, Bureau of the Census, *Census of Manufactures: 1905, Textiles, Bulletin* 74, 134–37.

17. A pamphlet, *Watkins Mill Guide* (Independence, Mo., n.d.), floor plans of the factory provided by the Missouri State Park Board,

Like all wools, the sacks of fleece obtained by the Watkins Mill from local storekeepers, by direct buying, or through orders to commission houses, varied in color, fineness, length, strength, and other qualities. The first operation, therefore, involved sorting lots into appropriate classes. Even the clips purchased from wool merchants, which were often presorted, needed separation and grading in accordance with the desired weight and quality of cloth. The next step was to clean the wool.

Typical of most pioneer mills, Watkins used a picking machine, which was a large rectangular box containing a revolving cylinder armed with spikes to knock out excess burrs and dirt. From the picking room, wool moved to the first floor, where both the washing and dyeing steps followed. Watkins's washers held an alkali-soap solution, and as the fleece moved in the machine, all dirt, grease, and vegetable matter went into suspension in the warm soapy water. Following several rinses and squeezings through ringers, the damp wool was hoisted to the fourth-floor drying room to be spread on racks. During July and August, workers on the fourth floor no doubt suffered from the intense heat and humidity, since wool in process was never allowed to dry completely.

Although Watkins apparently did not employ the process, some midwestern factories carbonized fleece. In carbonization, wool was immersed in a chemical solution of sulphuric acid and then heated to 160° F. With the application of heat, the chemical agent destroyed all extraneous matter without harming fleece fibers. Carbonizing proved especially necessary with wools containing an excessive number of burrs or where farmers had tied wool bundles with sisal twine.

Dyeing, which was handled on the first floor at Watkins, might take place at any one of several stages in the manufacturing process. Fleece could be dyed "in the wool," after its conversion to yarn, or by the piece as it came from the loom.

and correspondence with B. H. Rucker, Historical Administrator of the Watkins Mill State Park, aided the discussion of production processes in the Watkins Mill.

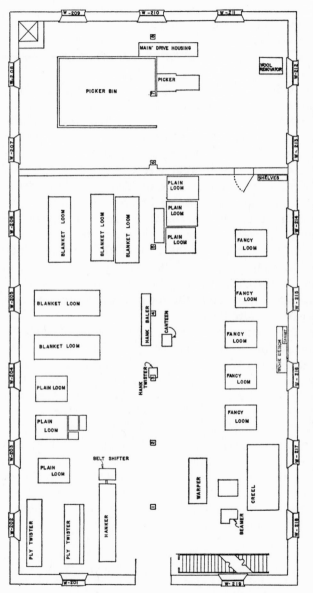

Second floor plan, Watkins Mill. Missouri State Park Board, Jefferson City.

The exact point chosen for the application of color varied with the type of wool and the finished pattern. Typical of other mills, Watkins possessed their own formulas, which were no doubt acquired from skilled artisans or through a long process of experimentation.

Carding involved straightening and intertwining long- and short-wool fibers in preparation for spinning. Wool taken from the fourth-floor drying racks at Watkins received a light application of oil to make it soft and pliable, and was then transported to the third-floor carding department. Each carding machine was equipped with a large revolving cylinder, flanked by smaller rollers, all of which were studded with short, wire teeth. Wool fed into the cards passed between the cylinders, which revolved in various directions. As a result, the brushed fleece formed a flat web, similar in appearance to a thin sheet of cotton batting. Rollers at the rear of the carding apparatus divided the web into several extended ropes, or rovings, which resembled yarn. After winding them on large spools, Watkins's card operators transferred the rovings to spinners on the opposite side of the third floor.

The fundamental principle of spinning was to extend and twist the rovings to create finished yarn. Like other factories in the Midwest, the Watkins Mill utilized machines on which the rovings were drawn and spun in the same operation. The rovings were threaded from the spindles, which were mounted on a movable carriage, through a set of pressure rollers, and then attached to the bobbins. The operator then moved the carriage outward, away from the bobbin rack, and simultaneously rotated a handcrank to activate the spindles. As the spindles revolved, the rovings were played out, while receiving the desired twist. A return of the carriage wound the twisted yarn on the bobbins, and the operator repeated the procedure. Continued trips of the carriage filled the bobbins, and the spinner then rethreaded.[18]

18. The hand-operated jack described in the Watkins spinning operation had become obsolete by the mid-1870s with the invention of the automatic mule. However, mills throughout the Midwest were slow to dispose of jacks and adopt the new technology.

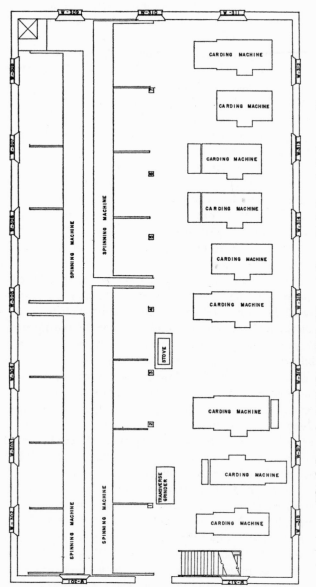

Third floor plan, Watkins Mill. Missouri State Park Board, Jefferson City.

Except for the need to twist several strands together, woolen yarn as it came from the spinning machines proved perfectly suitable for use as weft, or the crosswise filler threads employed in weaving. However, since power looms exerted great stress on the warp, or lengthwise threads, additional treatment of warp yarns was a necessity, and their preparation required three or four supplemental operations. Spools containing warp, which had usually received a tighter twist than weft, were arranged on the warper stand. At this point the selection of colors for future patterns began, since the dresser tender, as he was called, could arrange the various threads in numerous color combinations when he pulled them from the spools and laid them out on a large cylindrical wheel called the reel. A reverse rotation of the reel rewound the warp onto spools called loom beams. To impart greater strength, and to eliminate any protruding fibers, warp threads usually received an application of paste as they passed from the reel to the loom beam.

In harness weaving each warp thread was drawn off the loom beam, passed through a wire eyelet suspended in a wooden frame, and then fastened to another beam which took up the woven cloth. Weft yarn was wound on a bobbin and inserted in the shuttle, which moved back and forth thus weaving the weft over and under the warp. The reed, a horizontal wooden bar, slammed against the weft following each shuttle passage and kept the weave tight. The weaver's major duties with the power-driven harness loom were to watch for broken threads and to keep the shuttle filled.

Under ordinary circumstances woolen cloth fresh from the loom was not salable. Containing oil inserted prior to carding and paste applied before weaving, unfulled woolens were uneven in texture and often stiff and scratchy. The Watkins's fulling mill consisted of a hollow box with a water-tight compartment in its base, and was fitted with a set of pressure rollers in the upper portion. The fuller ran long pieces of cloth through the rollers, and sewed them end to end. When the machine started, the wet material was drawn up through the rollers, rung out, and then fell into the tub of warm, soapy water below.

Group of Faribault workers, ca. 1910.
Courtesy of the Faribault Woolen Mill.

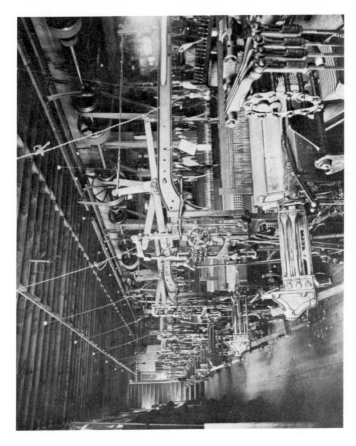

*Weave room, Faribault Woolen Mill, ca. 1906.
Courtesy of the Faribault Woolen Mill.*

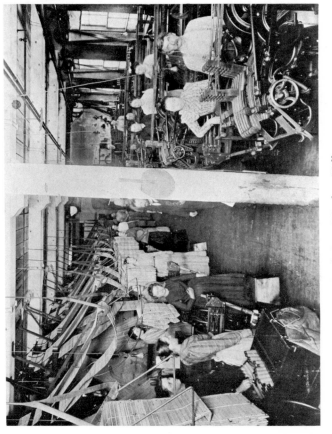

*Interior, North Star Woolen Mills, ca. 1910.
Courtesy of the Minnesota Historical Society.*

Carding machines, Watkins Mill.
Courtesy of the Missouri State Park Board.

Loom, reel, warper stand at Watkins Mill.
Courtesy of the Missouri State Park Board.

Watkins Mill, ca. 1910.
Courtesy of the State Historical Society of Missouri.

Rock River Woolen Mills, ca. 1907.
Courtesy of the State Historical Society of Wisconsin.

Appleton Mills, ca. 1893.
Courtesy of Appleton Mills.

Faribault Woolen Mill, 1967.

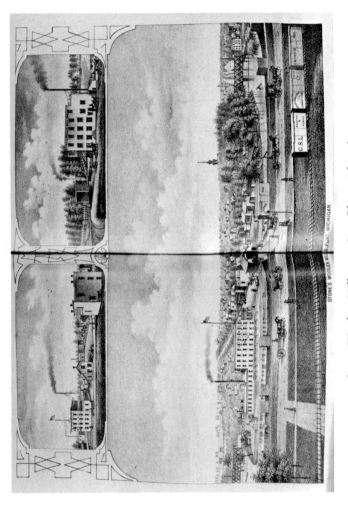

Stone Woolen Mill, ca. 1879. Photo taken from
pp. 136–37 of the History of Genesee County, Michigan.
Reproduction by the Michigan Historical Collections.

Fulling time depended on the type of fabric. The resulting cloth, shrunken to as much as one-third of its original size, received a rinse in clear water, and was then placed on racks to dry.

In the finishing department, dry cloth was napped and sheared, or pressed. Teazles, the spiny heads of a plant exactly the correct height to raise woolen nap, yet break off if embedded too far, had been employed in finishing woolen fabrics for centuries. With teazles set in a cylinder, Watkins's finisher slowly raised the nap, which he then cut to an even height with handscissors or a shearing machine. Flannel, an important item in the product line of most pioneer mills, required no shearing, as a steam press merely matted the nap.

Yarn for the retail trade moved from the spinning machines to a baler, hanker, and ply-twister located on the second floor. Yarns of several plies were formed by a twister, which pulled the threads from a rack filled with spools. After the hanker twisted yarn into hanks, the bundles were again twisted to prevent kinking and knotting in transit. A baler then compressed the hanks in order to save space, thus making shipment less expensive.

The sale of yarn to area residents who wished to knit and weave at home provided the bulk of receipts for some pioneer woolen concerns. Typical of such firms, mills in the Missouri towns of Carthage, Fulton, and Huntsville advertised their finished cloth in 1883, but all three strongly emphasized that woolen yarn represented the plant specialty.[19] As settlers continued to move westward, household wool manufacturing gradually gave way to factory production just as it had in the East, but domestic manufacturing continued to exist in the Midwest. Indeed, in more remote localities household spinners and weavers continued to operate their spinning wheels and handlooms alongside the complete factory as late as 1900. Therefore, at any given time, some of the fleece in process in a midwestern mill usually belonged to families in the immediate neighborhood availing themselves of the factory's custom services.

19. *Missouri State Gazetteer and Business Directory, 1883–1884* (St. Louis, Mo., 1884), 243, 357, 435.

A number of mills accepted raw wool for custom carding and spinning, and also fulled domestically woven cloth, while simultaneously fabricating their own material. The 1860 advertisement of Dale and McCoun, a woolen factory in Liberty, Missouri, amply illustrates the attempts of many mills to solicit business from household manufacturers. Through the local newspaper, the firm offered to do custom carding for eight cents per pound, or card, spin, and hank for twenty-five cents, in addition to producing their own cassimere, flannel, and yarn.[20] In its May 1870 sales flyer, Appleton Mills urged domestic cloth producers in Wisconsin to bring their wool and homespun fabrics to the plant in Appleton, assuring them that "cloth dressing and roll carding shall have our usual careful attention."[21]

Like the merchant, the pioneer wool manufacturer often found it necessary to accept farm produce in order to make sales and collect debts. The account book of the Corunna Woolen Mill in Michigan indicates that in 1866 the factory offered local customers alternative methods of payment for purchases of cloth and yarn. Pliny S. Lyman, the Corunna owner, took cash, raw wool, or a combination of both, processed the farmers' fleece and retained a portion as payment, or sold finished cloth in the fall and accepted personal notes promising "wool in the spring."[22] In addition to cash, fleece, and promissory notes, the Watkins Mill allowed Missouri farmers to pay with bacon, corn, dry hides, homemade soap, lard, wheat, and wood. Typical of other factories, the nonperishable products bartered to the Eagle Mills near Indianapolis were usually hauled to a larger market for disposal.[23]

20. *Liberty* (Mo.) *Weekly Tribune*, April 27 and June 8, 1860.

21. *Tenth Annual Circular of the Appleton Woolen Factory*, in the Appleton Collection.

22. Account Book, 1866, Corunna Woolen Mill, in the Pliny S. Lyman Papers, Michigan Historical Collections, University of Michigan, Ann Arbor.

23. *Liberty* (Mo.) *Tribune*, May 10, 1861, April 24, 1863; *Indianapolis Star*, August 9, 1942; *Indianapolis Sunday Star*, October 26, 1930.

Company stores offered several advantages for midwestern wool manufacturers. In some isolated areas the millstore comprised the only mercantile firm within several miles. Payrolls could sometimes be partially met with stock from store shelves, and the retailing of dry goods, hardware, and staple groceries provided profits to supplement those received from the sale of fabrics. Rural customers calling at the store for needed items might also be induced to buy cloth or yarn. The availability of mercantile goods, along with the willingness of most millowners to accept fleece in lieu of cash, no doubt prompted some farmers to market their wool clips at the local factory.

On a normal spring or summer day in the 1870s the average midwestern woolen mill bustled with trade activity. Farmers hauling wood, wool, and produce to the plant mingled with customers who came to examine finished goods in the factory showroom. Millowners encouraged both retail and wholesale buying at the plant. Rather than awaiting the arrival of salesmen, some local merchants visited mills directly to make personal selections, and since these visits reduced company expenses incurred in distribution, wool manufacturers invited prospective buyers to call at the mill. In Missouri, the Huntsville Woolen Mill provided storekeepers with transportation between the local rail depot and the factory sample rooms in the early 1880s. And, in its first newspaper advertisement in May 1861 the Watkins Mill hoped to increase its retail sales by urging ladies to inspect woolen fabrics at the plant, since they were "generally better judges than men, of such goods."[24]

To encourage further direct buying, some factories opened retail outlets in nearby towns or added special departments. The Faribault Mill, for example, established a showroom in Fergus Falls, Minnesota, in the spring of 1888.[25] Since many people took woolen cloth to local tailors to be fashioned into clothing, Hutchinson and Company of Appleton, Wisconsin, like a few

24. *Liberty* (Mo.) *Tribune,* May 10, 1861.
25. Frank H. Klemer, "The History of the Faribault Woolen Mills" (paper read before the Rice County, Minnesota, Historical Society, October 22, 1940, copy in the Minnesota Historical Society, St. Paul).

other mills, attempted to provide this service for their customers with the addition of a tailoring department to their salesroom in 1877. Through advertisements, Hutchinson's owners invited men and boys in the Appleton area to call at the company store, select material from a wide range of fabrics and styles, and to be fitted for a "good suit of clothes for $20."[26]

Direct buying at the factory generated some trade, but most mills sold the largest portion of their cloth and yarn through smalltown merchants, each of whom served residents in a tiny trade area of a few miles. As the middlewestern sheep population continued to increase after 1850, the region's rural storekeepers collected large quantities of fleece from local farmers in payment of accounts. Therefore, a mill-merchant exchange of raw wool for finished fabrics proved a mutually beneficial arrangement, and prior to the 1880s nearly every wool manufacturer in the Midwest utilized this method of sales.

The barter agreement worked out between the Island Woolen Mills at Baraboo and a storekeeper in Highland, Wisconsin, in April 1869 exemplifies the sales procedure of several pioneer wool manufacturers attempting to sell in the local market. Island's owners shipped a collection of fabric samples to David Ellsworth, the Highland merchant, along with a listing of ratios which indicated the pounds of wool to be taken in for each yard of cloth. Using the samples, Ellsworth then attempted to solicit fabric orders from farm families in the area who wished to sell their wool. When enough orders had been received, the fleece inventory was dispatched to Baraboo, the mill paying the freight charges on the wool from the store to the factory, and the farmers agreeing to pay the return freight on the finished product. As compensation, the Island Mills placed a monetary value on the finished cloth and Ellsworth collected a 10 percent selling commission.[27]

26. Advertisement in a pocket memorandum distributed by Hutchinson and Company, January 1, 1877, Appleton Collection.

27. In 1869, Island instructed merchants to barter one yard of fulled cloth for every two and two-thirds pounds of raw wool, and one yard of flannel for every two pounds. Island Woolen Mills, Baraboo, Wisconsin, to David Ellsworth, April 20, 1869, and P. E.

Over and above the assurance of finding adequate supplies of raw material, bartering finished cloth for wool helped in part to solve a major problem faced by all pioneer mills. Typical of most processors, the value added by wool manufacturers was relatively low, which meant that raw material constituted the largest single variable cost in woolen textile production. In some years fleece prices fluctuated wildly, but establishing a fixed ratio between fabrics and wool acted as a hedge against short-run price increases on raw material. Also, utilizing merchants who were willing to accept fleece eliminated the necessity of hiring a wool buyer or ordering from commission merchants, and the actual price the farmer received for his wool was hidden by the ratio. The strength of the barter system, however, rested upon each merchant's ability to grade fleece.

The methods employed to retail and wholesale cloth and yarn varied among mills, and some manufacturers preferred to extend credit to local merchants by placing fabric assortments in rural stores on a consignment basis, settling mercantile accounts once or twice each year. Merchants handling Watkins Mill cloth in the 1870s, for example, received sales commissions of 15 percent, with the option of returning all fabric remnants longer than three yards. The factory balanced accounts in January and July, with stock held by the storekeeper, plus sales commissions and any wool taken in for the mill then being deducted from the amount owed by the merchant.[28] Although no one store handled a large quantity of consigned cloth, a multitude of small firms did stock Watkins's goods. Thus, at any time, the factory had a substantial amount of money tied up in fabrics on mercantile consignment.[29]

Webster, February 11, 1869, in the Island Woolen Mills Collection, State Historical Society of Wisconsin, Madison.

28. For examples of such credit arrangements see the accounts of Royle and New, Ruben Puckett, and S. R. Crispin during 1876 in the Watkins Collection.

29. Inventory levels varied widely among stores. For example, the Watkins inventory of S. R. Crispin of Richmond, Missouri, amounted to only $28.18 in 1875, while in 1878, Royle and New, a Lexington, Missouri, mercantile concern, held Watkins's yarn and cloth valued at $913.97.

To deliver and collect cloth orders to and from rural stores, nearly all midwestern mills engaged traveling salesmen. Herman Belt, the Watkins Mill salesman in northwest Missouri during the 1870s, visited smalltown merchants within an approximate fifty-mile radius of the plant. Traveling by horse-drawn wagon, Belt collected accounts, delivered orders, displayed fabric samples, purchased raw wool, noted local business activity, ruled on credit extension, and, like all salesmen, received complaints. Although he had to revisit the factory every seven to ten days to replenish his supply of goods, to return cloth, and to unload fleece, Belt seems to have called on merchants in a four-county area on a regular basis. During November 1877, Belt conducted business with one or more stores in at least fifteen small Missouri towns.[30] In contrast to the Watkins technique, owners of the Island Woolen Mills in 1871 apparently issued fabric samples to many individuals who solicited orders in a random fashion, seeking mercantile customers wherever they could be found.[31]

The typical pioneer woolen mill usually limited sales to a small trade area, but by the 1890s a number of factories in the Midwest had closed their doors, and a few of those manufacturers who continued to operate tried to expand into the regional market. For example, in the winter of 1891 Appleton Mills in Wisconsin offered C. C. Hill six hundred dollars per year plus expenses to begin the sales of Appleton woolens in Lower Michigan.[32] Hill had previously traveled the territory as a

30. H. W. Belt, Note Book, 1877–1878, Wholesale and Retail Accounts, 1877–1878, and Personal Records, 1876–1877, in the Watkins Collection. In addition to supplying regular merchants, Watkins also furnished fabrics and yarn to Farmers' Grange Stores in several Missouri towns at the usual 15 percent sales commission.

31. By 1885, however, the Island Woolen Mills had abandoned retail sales to local merchants and concentrated all their efforts on selling to cloth jobbers and clothiers in Chicago, Cincinnati, Cleveland, and Detroit. James Balfour to the Island Woolen Mills, Chicago, March 6, 1885, Island Collection.

32. Appleton also employed two other salesmen who covered portions of Minnesota and Wisconsin, and in an effort to sell to garment makers in Chicago, the firm utilized Curtiss and Warren, selling agents in that city.

salesman for the woolen factory at Vassar, Michigan, which had ceased production the previous year, and because of his contacts in the area Appleton hoped that he could easily break into the new market. However, despite his friendship with local merchants, Hill found it extremely difficult to attract new customers. The small mills in Michigan could offer storekeepers fast service, frequently cut prices below those of Appleton, and occasionally postdated bills as much as five months in advance.[33]

Hill traveled from town to town by train, or hired a horse and buggy to reach those stores not adjacent to the railroad. In good weather he usually covered his entire route in five or six weeks. During sales trips, Hill informed Appleton of his actions, the general market conditions in the territory, and carefully watched the movements of other salesmen. He frequently sent samples of competitive cloth to Appleton for examination, and, if such material was selling well, Hill normally suggested that the factory try to produce a close copy at a cheaper price.[34]

Unlike some of his Michigan competitors, Hill did not sell goods on consignment, but offered merchants terms of 3/10, 1/30, net 60.[35] To stay in the market, Appleton found it necessary to give additional discounts to compensate for freight charges from Wisconsin to Michigan, and to make up special bolts of cloth less than the standard fifty yards. In an attempt to match the delivery speed of Michigan mills, Hill proposed the establishment of several storage depots along his sales route where Appleton fabrics and yarn could be stored in predetermined warehouses. The factory managers rejected the idea, however, no doubt because it necessitated a large inventory which might not sell at a profit.[36]

33. C. C. Hill to Appleton Mills, Grayling, Michigan, June 11, 1891, Appleton Collection.

34. Ibid., Vassar, Michigan, June 2, 5, and 8, 1891, and Saginaw, Michigan, June 11, 1891, Appleton Collection.

35. Two percent discount if paid within ten days, 1 percent if paid within thirty days, and the net amount when paid in sixty days.

36. C. C. Hill to Appleton Mills, Howell, Michigan, August 14, 1891, Sheboygen, Michigan, June 9, 1891, and Vassar, Michigan, September 15, 1891, Appleton Collection.

The interior transportation system of the Midwest in part delimited the sales area of the region's woolen mills. Service to rural stores demanded constant attention in order to maintain inventories of frequently purchased fabrics and to collect fleece taken in for factories. Except for those mills which could serve customers by rail, promptness of service was determined by the varying surface condition of country roads, often impassable in winter, and the speed of horse-drawn wagons. Even with the railroad, shipments were sometimes delayed. As late as 1881, a St. Louis merchant complained that it usually required six full days to receive woolen yarn sent by rail two hundred miles from a town in northwest Missouri.[37] Trade areas varied with local conditions. Flint Woolen Mills marketed the bulk of its products in southern Michigan towns, such as Albion, Battle Creek, Bellevue, Kalamazoo, and Jackson, all of which were within one hundred miles of the factory. Andrew Yount's mill in Indiana served residents as far away as sixty miles, while the Watkins Mill concentrated on selling fabrics and yarn in Missouri towns located inside a fifty-mile radius of the plant.

Prior to 1890, those woolen factories in the Middle West which confined sales activity to their immediate trade area seemed to have faced only limited competition from other mills within the region. A few storekeepers in the 1870s and 1880s grumbled about the high prices charged for cloth and yarn, but company records suggested that most merchants remained consistent customers of the same small mill year after year. Factory marketing by consignment, which built up store inventories on a credit basis, favorable terms such as delayed billing and discounts, and a storekeeper's close proximity to a wool manufacturer that could offer relatively speedy service reduced the probability of changing suppliers. Moreover, customer preferences, habit, and personal friendships with millowners shaped merchant attitudes. In memos to their employers, mill salesmen often blamed the inability to add new accounts on the blind devotion of a few stores to one particular woolen factory.

37. Case and Cabot Company to Watkins Mill, St. Louis, August 26, 1881, Watkins Collection.

Pioneer wool manufacturers attempted to entice customers near the factory or in surrounding small towns with two major types of advertising. Handbills, emphasizing the honesty of the owners and praising the skill of the workers, the elaborate and up-to-date machinery, and the high quality of fabrics produced, seemed popular with most millowners. Such flyers were distributed to area residents and merchants, and typical of the times and of this method, prices were seldom mentioned. To accentuate custom services, such as carding, fulling, and spinning, manufacturers also utilized the classified sections of weekly newspapers. Much like the merchants with whom they so often dealt, millowners repeatedly permitted an advertisement to run for several weeks without change. For example, during the early 1860s, the Dale Woolen Mill of Liberty, Missouri, continued the same advertisement in the *Liberty Tribune* for fourteen consecutive months.[38] Products of local woolen factories were also brought to public attention by storekeepers who listed such fabrics among items offered for sale. Illustrative of this procedure, an 1877 newspaper advertisement of Royle and New, a Lexington, Missouri, mercantile firm, noted the recent arrival of cloth and yarn from the Watkins Mill.[39] In 1891, salesmen for Appleton Mills placed placards in the windows of country stores, informing customers that good values could be found among the "Appleton Yarns, Flannels, Skirts, for Sale Here."[40]

With few exceptions, woolen mills in the Middle West faced serious shortages of funds to carry on normal business transactions. Consignment selling, extension of credit to merchants, and the need to purchase correct wool types when and where they were available, exerted pressure on millowners to acquire operating capital. Pioneer manufacturers paid higher interest rates on loanable funds than producers in the East, and under the National Banking system, western businessmen suffered each fall when country bankers expected prompt settlement of

38. *Liberty* (Mo.) *Tribune*, April 16, 1863, to June 24, 1864.
39. *The Lexington* (Mo.) *Intelligencer*, October 6, 1877.
40. C. C. Hill to Appleton Mills, Vassar, Michigan, June 5, 1891, Appleton Collection.

promissory notes. In the spring, banks advanced money to commission merchants to buy the new wool clip, and these firms normally sold to local mills on a credit of sixty days.[41] However, by July or early August wool dealers demanded payment since funds were now needed by local banks and other firms to finance the movement of farm produce which would hit the western market in the fall. For the same reason, country banks also forced woolen mills to settle accounts. Thus, midwestern wool manufacturers found money scarce and interest rates increasing at the very time when production was at its height and cloth sales at a minimum.[42]

After 1850 many eastern businessmen migrated westward to construct small woolen mills aimed at service to a local market, and by 1870 the Midwest contained 881 such factories.[43] A combination of high transportation costs on raw material and finished products provided these mills an advantage over manufacturers in the East on the sale of coarse- and medium-grade woolen textiles in the midwestern market. Custom-order services supplemented the income received from the sale of cloth and yarn. The typical pioneer factory faced capital shortages, or at best paid high interest rates, and constantly searched for skilled labor. The great distance to the eastern machinery market and the use of old equipment meant that the breakdown of a loom or the repair of a shearing machine might entail a temporary halt in production. Most mills could show a profit, however,

41. For a firsthand description of the movement of eastern bank capital into the West and South, see the *Commercial and Financial Chronicle* 7 (November 14, 1868): 615.

42. As one of many examples, in May 1874 the Ray County Savings Bank of Richmond, Missouri, notified the Watkins Mill that only one renewal would be allowed on its loan, and the interest rate on short term funds would increase after September 1, because "about that time money will be scarce." Ray County Savings Bank to Waltus Watkins, Richmond, Missouri, May 29, 1874, Watkins Collection. For other types of seasonal financial pressure on the same firm, see Benjamin McLean and Company, Kansas City, July 28, 1877, J. B. Carson Brothers, St. Louis, October 21, 1872, and E. Y. Moody, Edgerton, Missouri, July 3, 1877, to Watkins Mill, Watkins Collection.

43. *Census of Manufactures: 1905, Textiles,* 134–37.

as long as they produced fabrics best suited to local wool supplies and if they manufactured what rural and smalltown families wanted to buy. Since these firms were oriented to their local market any forces which affected that market threatened their very existence. Such forces developed within one generation.

CHAPTER VI

The Impingements
of a Nationalizing Market

In the long run, manufacturers commanding large capital resources can normally adjust production and distribution to compensate for changes in market demand, labor supplies, and raw material sources. Plants can be expanded or relocated, workers recruited from other regions, and shifts in consumer demand countered by adaptation of product lines. However, small firms possessing limited capital and only slight manufacturing and marketing advantages over other companies in an industry face the danger of extinction when unforeseen forces quickly transform the economic status quo. From the 1880s to 1920, midwestern woolen mills struggled to survive as fashion affected consumer preferences, improved transportation facilities altered markets, population shifted from rural to urban areas, and sheep moved farther westward.

In the decade before the Civil War, construction companies extended the American railroad network as far west as St. Joseph, Missouri, and La Crosse, Wisconsin, and by the early 1870s railroad bridges spanned the Mississippi and Missouri Rivers at four different locations.[1] Midwestern states and towns competed in further promotion, and as a result large portions of the region's population gained convenient and less expensive connections with the national market. Moreover, through the use of compromise cars, sliding wheels, and the addition of a third rail, the eight states of the Middle West had succeeded in coordinating track-gauge differentials by the turn of the century. Through bills of lading and reductions in freight rates then became possible since standardization eliminated the old necessity of loading and unloading shipments at each point where track gauges varied, or of hoisting cars to change wheels.[2]

In addition to steam railroads, midwestern residents enjoyed increased mobility from other sources. Ohio inaugurated the Midwest's first interurban railroad in 1888, and other states in the region soon launched similar programs. In 1915, over seven thousand miles of interurban track stretched through Illinois, Indiana, Michigan, and Ohio, while networks on a less grandiose scale extended through portions of Iowa, Missouri, and Wisconsin. The interurban concentrated on providing dependable, efficient, and rapid passenger service from small towns to larger cities. On normal runs, electrically powered interurban trains averaged thirty to thirty-five miles per hour, and in open country they were capable of reaching speeds as high as seventy to eighty miles per hour. Before the automobile brought their economic destruction after 1920, the interurban systems helped in part to alleviate the isolation of midwestern families.[3]

By comparison to its later impact, the passenger car had only begun to influence life in the Middle West by 1920. However, the rugged and relatively inexpensive Model T Ford, first offered to the public in 1908, seemed custom built to plow through the mud and ruts of country roads, and those people who could afford to purchase them found new trading centers beyond the local country store.[4] Car owners were soon pressuring state legislatures to construct and maintain better roads, and a Good Roads Movement gathered support from many people in the region. Michigan, for example, created a state highway depart-

1. Thomas C. Cochran, *Basic History of American Business* (Princeton, N.J., 1959), 59; Duane Meyer, *The Heritage of Missouri —A History* (St. Louis, Mo., 1963), 472–73.

2. George Rogers Taylor and Irene D. Neu, *The American Railroad Network, 1861–1890* (Cambridge, Mass., 1956), 35–41, 58–66, 83.

3. John F. Due, "The Rise and Decline of the Midwest Interurban," *Current Economic Comment* 14 (August 1952): 36–51.

4. Alfred D. Chandler, Jr., *Giant Enterprise: Ford, General Motors, and the Automobile Industry* (New York, 1964), 11–12.

ment in 1905, and within eight years the new agency had outlined a comprehensive road system. With the advent of automobiles, farmers also initiated campaigns for the rural free delivery of mail, much to the consternation of smalltown merchants who preferred that local residents purchase "at home," rather than buying from the new mail-order houses such as Sears, Roebuck and Montgomery Ward.[5]

Automobiles and better roads to drive them on, the interurban, along with expanded and improved rail service freed midwestern farmers and the citizens of rural small towns from economic and social isolation. Horse-drawn buggies and wagons no longer limited farmers to a journey of six to ten miles, and shopping trips to larger cities, on the interurban or in the family car, became more and more routine. Overcrowded coaches and rough, dusty roads no doubt discouraged a few people from all-day shopping excursions to the city, thereby allowing the rural merchant to continue to compete with department stores in larger urban centers, but the 24,000 items displayed in the 1890 Montgomery Ward catalog represented an added threat to country stores. Catalogs brought the city to the farmer's mailbox, and thus small storekeepers felt competitive pressure from mail-order houses since customers could easily compare prices.[6] Although both Sears and Wards demanded cash, whereas the local merchant extended credit, apparent savings might compensate for immediate monetary outlay. Woolen mill profits were linked directly to the prosperity of smalltown merchants, and after 1890 wool manufacturers saw the volume of fabric sales to such firms slowly dwindle each year.

5. Sidney Glazer, "The Rural Community in the Urban Age: The Changes in Michigan since 1900," *Agricultural History* 23 (April 1949): 131; Lewis E. Atherton, *Main Street on the Middle Border* (Bloomington, Ind., 1954), 231–33.

6. Montgomery Ward and Company, founded in 1872 by Aaron M. Ward, was Chicago's first large mail-order house. Sears, Roebuck and Company, established in 1886, moved to Chicago in 1895. Boris Emmet and John Jeuck, *Catalogues and Counters: A History of Sears, Roebuck and Company* (Chicago, 1950), 19; Atherton, *Main Street*, 231.

The development of mature banking and marketing systems in the Middle West during the last quarter of the nineteenth century also freed farmers from their previous dependence upon country stores to extend credit and to market produce. Better and cheaper transportation opened the grain and live-stock markets of Kansas City, Chicago, Minneapolis, and St. Louis, and as the Northeast continued to industrialize, increasing demand for western farm staples expanded rural incomes. In addition, a growing number of farmers abandoned the feed-lot and plow to seek jobs within the region in automotive assembly, flour milling, processing forest products, and meat-packing. In the twenty years after 1880, average personal per capita income increased in the Midwest by approximately $120, and with more money to spend consumers insisted on both a wider variety of manufactured goods and products of better quality.[7]

While disposable incomes grew and rural mobility increased, the Midwest's population exploded and moved to town. By 1900, the region contained over twenty-three million inhabitants, a gain of nearly seven million in twenty years, and the number of evacuees from farming to industry matched the intensity of the boom in total population. In 1880, 20 percent of all midwesterners resided in a town of four thousand or more people—ten years later, 33 percent. Rural-city emigration varied within the region, but during the 1880s central Missouri, eastern Iowa, northern and western Illinois, along with the southern sections of Indiana, Michigan, and Ohio experienced heavy losses in farm residents.[8] By the turn of the century more than one-half of the labor force in every midwestern state except Iowa was earn-

7. Simon Kuznets and others, *Population Redistribution and Economic Growth, 1870–1950*, 3 vols. (Philadelphia, 1960), 2: 185.

8. U.S. Department of Commerce, Census Office, *Abstract of the Twelfth Census, 1900* (Washington, D.C., 1902), 32; Conrad Taeuber, "Rural-Urban Migration," *Agricultural History* 15 (July 1941): 157; Arthur M. Schlesinger, *The Rise of the City, 1878–1898* (New York, 1933), 57, 67. On the national level, the urban population grew by 4 percent a decade from 1840 to 1880, and by 6 percent from 1880 to 1900. Alfred D. Chandler, Jr., *Strategy and Structure: Chapters in the History of Industrial Enterprise* (Garden City, N.J., 1966), 27.

ing the majority of its income from nonagricultural pursuits.[9]

For the region's wool manufacturers such demographic changes spelled disaster. The growth in the Midwest's population from 1870 to 1900 enlarged the total regional market, but, paradoxically, the migration of farmers to urban centers decreased the market of most pioneer mills. Since woolen factories had previously concentrated on selling cloth and yarn to nearby farmers and the residents of small towns, the exodus of people from these areas sharply reduced the total number of potential customers. The volume of fabric sales fell, custom orders declined, and the country stores and the woolen mill that supplied their cloth inventories could look to the future and only anticipate a continuation of the same trend. And, by 1900, selling in the larger cities of the Middle West meant competing with cloth producers in the East.

Transportation charges on eastern manufactures shipped to the Middle West declined steadily during the 1870s and 1880s, and in the process woolen mills in the region lost a substantial portion of their previous protection from eastern competitive fabrics. Freight rates on dry goods moved by rail from New York to St. Louis fell from $1.50 per hundred pounds in 1870 to $0.87 in 1900; New York to Chicago, from $1.13 to $0.75; and, New York to Detroit, from $0.88 to $0.59 cents. Charges for short hauls also exhibited marked declines. For example, the average rate per ton mile on the Michigan Central was cut 75 percent in the thirty years after 1870.[10] Eastern woolen factories and western consumers might rejoice at lower transportation costs, but to woolen mills in the Midwest each reduction increased the danger of competition from outside the region. Some pioneer wool manufacturers fretted over the possibility of cheap textiles flooding the local market, but in a few years a major change in fashions closely connected with urbanization

9. Kuznets, *Population Redistribution*, 2: 82.

10. H. T. Newcomb, *Changes in the Rate of Charge for Railroads and Other Transportation Services*, United States Department of Agriculture, Div. of Stat., Misc. ser., *Bulletin 15*, 22, 37–38, 42. In general, Boston shipments to the Midwest paid the same freight charges as those originating in New York.

made the entire question of East-West freight rates irrelevant.

Many factors contribute to the emergence of fashion in a particular society, but once individuals congregate in groups, such as cities and towns, personal appearance assumes increased importance. The social phenomenon labeled fashion is both a quest for novelty and a desire for conformity. A high degree of fashion or style consciousness usually develops in cultures possessing a large, affluent middle class which places heavy emphasis on material gratification. For a few, wearing the "latest thing" provides a temporary status symbol because not all members of the group can afford to discard or alter clothing each year, while for many it merely represents conforming to the current seasonal mode of dress in order to appear like others.[11] As American cities and towns grew in number and in population during the 1880s and 1890s, the desire for fashion in garments increased. Except for the meager amounts utilized for upholstering material, woolen textiles entered few industrial or domestic markets, and an overwhelming majority of these fabrics went into clothing. Therefore, fashion in wearing apparel injected the woolen industry with a highly unstable element because by 1900 style and readymade clothing had become synonymous.

Enterprising businessmen in New York City began factory production of ready-to-wear clothing in the early 1830s, and despite the panic later in the decade, within fifteen years the industry was well established in the East. Most early factories merely sold cut-up material, which local women then stitched together in their own homes. Although the number of such plants grew rapidly, they offered only limited competition to custom-tailors who continued to produce the bulk of men's garments until 1865. The introduction of the sewing machine in the 1850s increased the rate of sewing to as much as nine

11. Dwight E. Robinson, "Fashion Theory and Product Design," *Harvard Business Review* 36 (November–December 1958): 127, and "The Importance of Fashion in Taste to Business History: An Introductory Essay," *Business History Review* 37 (Spring–Summer 1963): 13–14. Also see Paul H. Nystrom's discussion of the psychology of fashion in his study *Economics of Fashion* (New York, 1928).

hundred stitches per minute, but it was government demand caused by the Civil War which actually placed men's ready-mades on a firm economic foundation. Huge orders for army uniforms encouraged plant construction and expansion, and military needs necessitated the standardization of sizes.[12]

Consumers in the postbellum period quickly began to appreciate the convenience and value of ready-to-wear, and by 1869 over seven thousand factories concentrated on manufacturing such clothing. After the Civil War the heavy influx of unskilled immigrants provided a large pool of labor, and by the turn of the century Jews from Austria, Germany, and Russia dominated the industry. During the 1870s and 1880s the contract system became popular, in which manufacturers sent cut-up cloth to small contractors whose workers each performed a small portion of fabrication. Cheap labor, the large number of hand operations, and the added influence of fashion in clothing confined the ready-to-wear industry to small shops. Frequent style changes prevented bulk purchases of fabrics, since material could not be safely carried over from one season to the next, and demands for different designs retarded the use of machines in the cutting operation. As late as 1890 less than 10 percent of all garment shops contained power equipment.[13]

Because of the city's close proximity to the New England textile mills, and since most imported fabrics entered its port, New York continued to maintain its hold on the garment industry, and in a short time was recognized as the nation's leading fashion center. By 1900, garment manufacturers in the New York suburban area accounted for nearly one-half of the ready-made clothing produced in the United States. Although the

12. Edna Bryner, *The Garment Trades* (Cleveland, Ohio, 1916), 13; "War as a Stimulus to American Industry," *Bulletin of the Business Historical Society* 8 (January 1934): 51.

13. J. M. Budish and George Soule, *The New Unionism in the Clothing Industry* (New York, 1927), 16–24; Florence S. Richards, *The Ready-to-Wear Industry, 1900–1950* (New York, 1951), 7–8. Except where brand names could be promoted, large firms possessed few advantages over small ready-to-wear manufacturers. The numerous hand operations reduced the optimum-size plant and prevented additional economies of scale in large factories.

industry experienced a phenomenal growth in Chicago, Cincinnati, and Philadelphia, New York City had lost only a small percentage of its dominant position twenty years later. Women's ready-to-wear, which developed somewhat later than the men's sector, also localized in the East, with New York's garment district turning out approximately 75 percent of the country's output in 1920.[14]

Many consumers in the Middle West had been introduced to readymade garments long before they revolutionized American textile markets. In the 1830s, St. Louis merchants were advertising eastern-manufactured suits for men and boys, and within twenty years stores in several other midwestern cities displayed such wearing apparel.[15] The scent of large profits through clothing sales to the western market lured a host of small garment makers to Chicago and Cincinnati. As early as 1851, officials in the latter city reported that over nine thousand women were currently employed in 108 garment factories.[16]

In an effort to reach the expanding national market, eastern manufacturers employed display advertising in newspapers and in magazines such as *Scribner's*, *Harper's*, and the *Atlantic*. Such advertisements increased by over 75 percent in the 1880s and went on to grow another one-third in the 1890s.[17] Department stores also arrived in the larger cities of the Midwest during the 1890s, bringing with them a one-price policy, the money-back guarantee, and special departments featuring the

14. Mabel A. Magee, *Trends in Location of the Women's Clothing Industry* (Chicago, 1930), 111–14; Jesse Pope, *The Clothing Industry in New York*, University of Missouri Studies, no. 1, (Columbia, Mo., 1905) 1: 288–92; Harold Underwood Faulkner, *The Decline of Laissez Faire, 1897–1917* (New York, 1951), 145.

15. Wayland A. Tonning, "The Beginnings of the Money-Back Guarantee and the One Price Policy in Champaign-Urbana, Illinois, 1833–1880," *Business History Review* 30 (June 1956): 199; Lewis E. Atherton, "Early Western Mercantile Advertising," *Bulletin of the Business Historical Society* 12 (September 1938): 52.

16. *Preliminary Report of the Eighth Census, 1860*, in Guy Stevens Callender, *Selections from the Economic History of the United States, 1765–1860* (Boston, 1909), 481.

17. Edward C. Kirkland, *Industry Comes of Age: Business, Labor, and Public Policy, 1860–1897* (New York, 1961), 272.

latest eastern clothing fashions.[18] Not to be slighted, farmers could view current styles on advertising material mailed to storekeepers by garment manufacturers. And, of course, mail-order houses encouraged farmwomen to abandon dresses made at home and to don the latest factory-made fashions on Sunday and for special occasions. Consumers were being told that what had once sufficed for clothing on the farm was somehow no longer acceptable in town.[19] Certainly by 1920, fashion and readymade clothing were fast becoming almost as much a part of midwestern life as cattle, corn, and conservative politics.

The switch from homemade to readymade clothing relocated the market of most midwestern mills. Within twenty years wool manufacturers in the region lost all previous advantages arising from a close proximity to the market. When rural families migrated to the city, the mills' market moved with them from country stores in the immediate vicinity of the plant to the newly populated urban centers. And the fashion trend favoring ready-to-wear again shifted the locus of demand—in the second instance, several hundred miles from the Middle West to the Atlantic Coast. Eastern garment makers, rather than the residents of midwestern farms and towns, comprised the most important consumers of woolen fabrics by 1900. Thus, as a result of fashion and urbanization, woolen textiles had been converted from a consumer good to a raw product.

Furnishing coarse woolen cloth to customers in the Middle West who sewed their own clothing at home was one thing, but attempting to supply fine-quality fabrics to hundreds of tiny garment shops located in larger cities was quite another. Instant knowledge of style changes, the daily actions and prices of competitors, and the mood of buyers in the market at any given time constituted the very minimum of information necessary to sell in the garment districts. The ease and speed with which a small textile factory might convert from the production of one type of material to another could perhaps offer important man-

18. For a discussion of their growth in one midwestern state, see Wayland A. Tonning, "Department Stores in Down State Illinois, 1889–1943," *Business History Review* 29 (December 1955): 335–49.
19. Atherton, *Main Street*, 227–28.

ufacturing cost advantages over larger concerns, but because mills in the Middle West were isolated they were more out of touch with fashion changes than firms close to the clothing market. Capital scarcity prohibited many pioneer manufacturers from employing the best, and therefore the most expensive, merchandising agents; the ability of experienced selling agents to sense subtle changes in the market and to predict its future direction, gave mills who could afford to purchase their services the upper hand over others in the trade.[20] In addition to these problems, a shortage of skilled labor, along with the homemade, secondhand, and obsolete machinery collected over a number of years, prevented all but a very few midwestern mills from producing woolen fabrics of high quality, or at a price low enough to permit competition with up-to-date factories. The limitations of capital, expertise, machinery, and labor also thwarted these firms from supplying garment makers within their own region in Chicago, Cincinnati, Cleveland, and St. Louis.

Those millowners in the Midwest who ventured into the eastern textile market during the 1890s were immediately struck with the realization that wool manufacturers in that region had been struggling for a number of years with competitors from another branch of the industry. Affluence, better heated homes, urban living, and, later, the closed automobile, prompted many Americans in the postbellum period to demand lighter and more stylish fabrics than those produced by most woolen concerns. Thus, as early as the 1870s fashion-conscious consumers in the East had started to favor worsted material. Clothing customers could readily identify cloth woven from worsted yarn by the evident weave pattern, light weight, and hard, lustrous finish. Suits of all-wool worsted with their clean-cut lines had become the vogue in men's dress by 1890.[21]

20. Hansjorg Siegthaler critically analyzes the economic contribution of dry goods commission houses in "What Price Style? The Fabric-Advisory Function of the Drygoods Commission Merchant, 1850–1880," *Business History Review* 41 (Spring 1967): 36–61.

21. Herman E. Michl, *The Textile Industries: An Economic Analysis* (Washington, D.C., 1938), 197.

Woolen and worsted manufacturing differed primarily in the processes employed prior to spinning. Wool for worsted yarn was carded, then passed through a series of mechanical combs which removed all short ends, straightened the remaining fibers, and laid them parallel to each other. They were then spun very tightly.[22] Since worsted combs parallelized all fibers, wool passed through them had to be long enough to permit such an operation. Commercially, worsted manufacturing had its beginning in the United States with the Canadian Reciprocity Treaty of 1854, which allowed the duty-free importation of fleece suitable for combing. While the woolen industry experienced a general trend toward geographic dispersion immediately after the Civil War, worsted mills remained in the East, close to capital markets and the major cities which imported foreign fleece. The invention of an improved combing machine in 1888, capable of handling short-fibered wool, plus crossbreeding by American sheep raisers, freed worsted manufacturers from complete dependence upon imports for raw material.[23] However, close proximity to the readymade clothing industry and the large capital investment in plant and machinery encouraged worsted mills to stay in New England.[24]

Worsted factories enjoyed several important cost advantages over woolen mills. A large number of automatic machines permitted the employment of unskilled labor in most departments, and market demand allowed high-volume production of a few staple-grade fabrics, such as serge, at very low cost. Moreover,

22. A complete description of worsted manufacturing can be found in A. F. DuPlessis, *The Marketing of Wool* (London, 1931), 22–46.

23. Despite such improvements, domestic production of combing wool lagged well behind domestic demand for many years. For example, in 1905, combing wool imports for consumption exceeded twenty million pounds. Chester W. Wright, *Wool-Growing and the Tariff* (Cambridge, Mass., 1910), 343.

24. The additional steps in production before spinning necessitated a heavy capital investment in complicated and expensive combing machines. For that reason, the investment in a worsted factory was normally much larger than the investment in a woolen mill. Modern machinery and the mixture of wool with snythetic fibers all but eliminated the once important distinction between woolen and worsted fabrics.

combed wool, or "top," could be classified into standard grades and traded in a futures market, something impossible with carded fleece. In less than twenty years, 1880 to 1899, the value of worsted fabrics produced in the United States increased by approximately eighty-seven million dollars; by the close of the period worsteds had surpassed woolens as the major branch of the industry.[25] While woolen and worsted manufacturers fought for the allegiance of consumers in the East, millowners out in the Midwest were observing a new threat to their existence— the exodus of sheep from the region.

Population pressure and rising land values after 1870 forced many farmers in the Midwest to abandon sheep in favor of heavier concentration on cereals, beef and pork production, and dairy farming. Never completely committed to woolgrowing as a commercial enterprise, cornbelt farmers tended to dispose of flocks when fleece prices declined and sheep raising failed to pay as well as other agricultural pursuits. In more densely populated areas packs of stray dogs exacted a heavy annual toll of flocks, but, no doubt reacting to public pressure, most midwestern legislators generally remained reluctant to enact statutes aimed at restricting the mobility of man's best friend. As sheep lost the battle of comparative advantage, the Midwest's ovine population tumbled. Less than one-fourth of the thirty-nine million sheep in the United States in 1900 could be found in the Middle West, and in that year the federal census enumerated only 8,500,000, a decline of approximately five million in thirty years.[26]

Because of their hardiness, a strong propensity to flock, and an amazing ability to forage and survive in rugged, arid regions, Merinos seemed ideally suited for the dry, open country

25. Arthur Harrison Cole, "A Neglected Chapter in the History of Combinations: The American Wool Manufacture," *Quarterly Journal of Economics* 37 (May 1923): 439; L. D. H. Weld, "Specialization in the Woolen and Worsted Industry," *Quarterly Journal of Economics* 27 (November 1912): 70–71.

26. U.S. Department of Commerce, Bureau of the Census, Eleventh Census, *Agriculture: 1890*, 92–93, and Thirteenth Census, *Agriculture*, 5: 407.

of the West. And like cattlemen, sheep owners soon perceived the economic advantages of utilizing the public domain for grazing. The violent conflicts between cowboys and sheepherders during the 1870s and 1880s merely indicated that midwestern sheep were pouring onto ranges of the Far West in ever-increasing numbers. As only one example of the trend, Montana's sheep population jumped from a few thousand in 1870 to over four million in 1900, elevating that state to the nation's top in sheep production.[27]

Sheep in the Middle West not only declined in total numbers, but farmers shifted from woolgrowing to the production of mutton for sale to the meatpackers of Chicago, Kansas City, and Omaha. As a result, they quickly exchanged the Merino, with its small frame, for one of the crossbreeds, such as the Shropshire, which combined a large carcass of high food value with a medium-quality fleece. Crossbred sheep, however, usually yielded coarser wool and in much smaller quantities than the Merino, and buyers often discounted clips from such animals because the black wool from the feet, head, and legs tended to mix with white fibers, thereby sharply reducing its utility to manufacturers.[28] As early as 1875, the *Minneapolis Daily Tribune* warned Minnesota farmers that they were making a serious mistake by giving up Merinos in favor of the coarse-wooled breeds,[29] and in 1909 an owner of the Flint Woolen Mills complained to a close friend that Michigan fleece was no longer suitable for manufacturing because "there appears to be a great many coarse locks and streaks . . . and they appear to be very kempy. . . . It is very seldom you will find a flock in Michigan, even in a small way, that will run as uniform as a flock of Western sheep."[30] Typical of all states in the

27. *Thirteenth Census, Agriculture*, 5: 407.
28. American Sheep Producers Council, *Breeds of Sheep*, Educational Pamphlet 3 (Denver, Colo., n.d.), passim.
29. *Minneapolis Daily Tribune*, August 15, 1875.
30. Flint Woolen Mills to M. J. Smiley, Flint, Michigan, April 26, 1909, in the Stone-Atwood Company Records, Michigan Historical Collections, University of Michigan, Ann Arbor. Kempy wool contained fibers called "kemps" which would not absorb solutions, thus

Midwest, Indiana listed only five counties in 1900 containing a substantial number of Merinos, nearly all its woolgrowers having shifted to the fattening of western lambs.[31]

As the popularity of wool as a market commodity disappeared in the Middle West, eastern commission merchants closed their branch offices in the region, while several midwestern wool dealers sought investments in more lucrative areas. Many local produce speculators, so important in an earlier period in finding and collecting small lots of fleece, focused their attention on other agricultural products. With many of these middlemen gone or inactive, and faced with a declining wool clip, few midwestern mills could afford the convenience and luxury of several direct buyers. Woolen factories which continued to operate found it more and more necessary to procure raw material from woolhouses in larger cities, and by 1914 Boston alone handled 70 percent of all the wool marketed in the United States.

Millowners came to rely upon commission merchants for another reason. Since the vagaries of fashion might change the demand for different types of wool, small mills without several buyers had to depend upon woolhouses who purchased and stored various grades of fleece awaiting orders. Manufacturers caught holding large wool inventories could suffer heavy financial losses if the preferences of consumers in the clothing market shifted suddenly; buying clips before styles and prices had been well established proved exceedingly risky. Some mills in the East received special freight rates on wool moved by rail from terminals on the Pacific Coast to Boston, which represented a lower rate than the freight charges on fleece shipped from interior points. Thus, from a monetary standpoint, a few eastern wool manufacturers by 1920 were closer to the domestic wool supply than mills located in the Midwest.

As soon as the Middle West joined the national market, wool

manufacturers could not use such fleece for fabrics dyed in solid colors.

31. Edward Norris Wentworth, *America's Sheep Trails, History, Personalities* (Ames, Iowa, 1948), 161.

manufacturers in the region inherited all the problems of the industry on the national level. The demand for worsted material and the movement of sheep to the Far West only compounded the instability created by consumer demands for readymade clothing. Midwestern mills attempting to sell textiles in the East faced competition from both woolen and worsted manufacturers, many of whom enjoyed access to relatively large capital resources, operated modern, well-equipped factories, and disposed of output through aggressive, experienced selling agents. Gone were the days when pioneer millowners could run machinery at their leisure, when retailing meant serving farmers and their wives at the counter of the company store, and when wholesaling involved horse-and-wagon deliveries of a few miles to rural and smalltown merchants. Faced with declining local demand for piece goods and yarn, most of the older woolen men simply closed the doors of their factories, accepting what appeared to be the inevitable. However, a few businessmen continued to search for possible solutions to their plight.

CHAPTER VII

The Struggle for Survival

The economic and social undercurrents of urbanization compelled most midwestern wool manufacturers to abandon their business sometime during the last quarter of the nineteenth century. Progress exacted its toll and within two generations vacant mills dotted the countryside, providing older residents with memories of an era when country stores were the center of trade, sheep abounded in the area, and horses provided transportation. In the thirty years after 1870 the midwestern woolen industry suffered an average of twenty-three mill failures per year. The region's 881 factories in 1870 dwindled to only 183 by 1900, and all but a few of the seventy mills which remained in 1920 had long since abandoned the manufacture of woolen fabrics for apparel.[1]

An examination of the different courses of action taken by four midwestern woolen concerns after 1870 illustrates a number of the possible alternatives open to such firms in their efforts to avert failure. The methods employed by the managers of the Watkins Mill in Missouri, the Faribault Mill in Minnesota, Flint Woolen Mills in Michigan, and the Appleton Mills of Wisconsin offer insights into some of the problems confronting small companies forced to enter the national market during this period. Moreover, case studies of these four mills strongly suggest that the degree of perception exhibited by managers and owners frequently plays a significant role in business success.

Following its construction in 1861, the owner of the Watkins Mill, located near Lawson, Missouri, marketed the bulk of factory output by placing yarn and fabric assortments in small-town stores within fifty miles of the plant. Additional income from a factory salesroom and company store, a flour-and-grist mill, and custom carding and spinning supplemented profits from consignment sales. Waltus Watkins, the mill's founder, accepted farm produce, wood, and wool in payment for cloth, flour and meal, or custom services, and procured the bulk of the firm's raw material through direct purchases from woolgrowers in northwest Missouri. Watkins divided his time between wool manufacturing and a rather extensive farming and livestock operation, sometimes closing the mill during the winter months when inclement weather hindered its operation.

By the early 1880s, when the elder Watkins retired and his three sons assumed control of the business, cloth sales to rural stores had already started to decline and farmers in that section of Missouri were rapidly disposing of fine-wooled Merinos. While maintaining service to local merchants, Judson, John, and Joseph Watkins expanded the mill's output of yarn, and negotiated contracts for the delivery of such goods to several large mercantile firms in Kansas City, St. Joseph, and St. Louis.[2] Extant records do not clearly indicate all the problems, but it seems obvious from correspondence that the Watkins brothers lacked even their father's meager commitment to wool manufacturing, and that sales of fabrics and yarn failed to yield profits in sufficient quantity to justify updating equipment, or for that matter, continuing production for an extended period of time. The factory carded raw wool for local farmers and family friends for a number of years,[3] and periodically manufactured some cloth, but for all practical purposes the Watkins Mill had ceased to be a viable business enterprise by 1886. In 1900, John Watkins confessed to the Director of the Census that plant machinery had been idle for several years, was in

1. U.S. Department of Commerce, Bureau of the Census, Fourteenth Census, *Manufacturing, 1919*, 10: 264–65, and *Census of Manufactures: 1905, Textiles*, Bulletin 74, 134–36.

2. Three letters, John Watkins to Judson Watkins, St. Louis, all dated September 13, 1883, and Bullene, Moore, and Emery to Watkins Mill, Kansas City, October 27, 1880, in the Watkins Mill Collection, Jackson County, Missouri, Historical Society, Archives, Independence.

3. M. Wilson to John Watkins, Ludlow, Missouri, September 4, 1902, Watkins Collection.

need of repair, and that his workers had all gone elsewhere, because "I run the farm and neglect the mill."[4]

As early as 1882 the Watkins brothers had entertained the possibility of moving the mill farther west.[5] The Fort Worth, Texas, Board of Trade contacted John Watkins and the owner of a woolen mill in Iowa, in an attempt to induce one or both firms to relocate in that community. Watkins corresponded with Fort Worth representatives, sent fabric samples for exhibition to potential investors there, and personally visited the city to discuss details with local officials. At first, Fort Worth promoters appeared interested in the plan, but soon expressed concern regarding the age of the machinery in the Watkins Mill, and the proposal failed to materialize.[6]

During the fall of 1884, John Watkins again visited the West, this time to survey parts of New Mexico as a possible site for the relocation of the mill. Following his visit to Albuquerque, John seemed pleased with what he had seen, and in a letter to his brother Judson in early October, he outlined the reasons for his optimism: "We called on the land agent for the Atlantic and Pacific R.R. and . . . [he] thinks a mill located here would be a good thing. He says the Pueblo Indians could be used in the mill and at very low wages. The people here say the Pueblos are the best workers in the country. Fuel would be high and hard to get however there is plenty of coal about 15 miles from here . . . , the A. and P. R. R. when extended East will run through it. . . . Wool is worth 9 to 10 cts per lb."[7] John's observations produced

4. John Watkins to the Director of the Twelfth Census, Lawson, Missouri, May 16, 1900, Watkins Collection.

5. In 1874, owners of the Watkins Mill had received inquiries concerning the removal of the woolen factory to Leavenworth, Kansas. See E. Estes to John Watkins, Leavenworth, January 1, 1874, Watkins Collection.

6. W. P. Wilson to John Watkins, Fort Worth, August 14, 1882, and October 9, 1882, Watkins Collection; Wilson, Paddock and Company to M. D. Scruggs, Fort Worth, June 26, 1882, and June 27, 1882, and M. D. Scruggs to John Watkins, Fort Worth, July 30, 1882, copies in the private collection of Mrs. Ruth B. Roney, Lawson, Mo.

7. John Watkins to Judson Watkins, Albuquerque, October 9, 1884, in the private collection of Mrs. Manfred Weber, Shawnee Mission, Kansas.

little action and this venture also resulted in disappointment. Actually, relocation in a new frontier area would only have delayed the inevitable for a few more years. As soon as New Mexico had developed adequate internal transportation and had joined the national market, Watkins's problems would have reappeared.[8]

While the owners of the Watkins Mill in Missouri looked to the west, farther north in Minnesota the managers of the Faribault Woolen Mill were just starting to experience similar problems. The woolen factory in Faribault had its beginning when Carl Klemer, a German immigrant and cabinetmaker by trade, purchased a used, horsepowered carding machine in 1865. Two years later, a small steam engine replaced the treadmill, and in 1872 Klemer added spinning jennies for the production of yarn. Despite capital shortages and three disastrous fires within four years, Klemer managed to continue expansion as dyeing vats, looms, and other appliances were included to make a complete factory. By the early 1890s, the company owned a two-set mill with up-to-date machinery, and the blankets, cassimeres, and flannels manufactured at Faribault typified the output of a hundred other mills in the Midwest.[9]

Carl Klemer's two sons, Henry and Ferdinand, entered the business as managers and partners during the 1890s, just in time to witness the decline of fabric sales to consumers in Minnesota and to feel the increased competition from ready-made clothing. To reach this new market, the owners installed sewing machines in one department of the plant in 1901 and shifted part of the labor force to production of men's all-wool pants and shirts. In an effort to obtain additional funds, the business was incorporated in 1905, and the following year

8. The Watkins Mill is located approximately seven miles west of Lawson, Missouri, in Ray County. The Missouri State Park Board opened the mill and plantation to the public in 1966.

9. The discussion of the early history of the Faribault Mill is based on Frank H. Klemer, "The History of the Faribault Woolen Mills" (paper read before the Rice County, Minnesota, Historical Society, October 22, 1940, copy in the Minnesota Historical Society, St. Paul), and "Large Midwestern Woolen Mill Founded by German Cabinetmaker," *America's Textile Reporter* 75 (June 8, 1961): 47–49, 58.

capital stock was offered to the general public and to the Minneapolis selling agent who marketed the firm's products. Experiencing little success in the ready-to-wear trade, the managers discontinued the sale of clothing and turned men and machines to the manufacture of quality blankets.

After working several years in other woolen factories and completing a course of study at the Philadelphia Textile School, Walter Klemer, a grandson of the founder, joined the company in 1912. Almost immediately Walter intensified the specialization on all-wool, fine-quality blankets, while sharply curtailing the production of piece goods and yarn. Orders for 100,000 army blankets plus a government wool allotment sustained the mill through World War I, and by 1920 Faribault blankets were being sold in large department stores throughout the country and to hospitals, hotels, and other public and private institutions. Concentration on blankets permitted internal economies of scale stemming from high-volume production, eliminated the need to search for different types of wool with each caprice of fashion, and avoided the instability of the garment industry.

Perhaps because of its location in the heart of a rapidly industrializing area, the owners of the Flint Woolen Mills of Flint, Michigan, were forced to search for a competitive position in one sector of the woolen industry somewhat earlier than most mills in the Midwest. Oren Stone, a farmer, merchant, and real estate speculator, constructed the factory at Flint in 1867 to utilize Lower Michigan's abundant wool supply and to offer the growing population in the southern portion of the state coarse- and medium-quality blankets, flannels, and jeans.[10] Although several partners entered and left the business from time to time, Stone personally supervised both production and sales until 1900. Typical of such firms, he emphasized custom carding and spinning during the early years of the operation.[11]

Quickly sensing the future importance of readymade cloth-

10. Stone first organized the business as Stone-Atwood Company, but in 1900 new owners renamed it the Flint Woolen Mills.
11. *Biographical History of Genesse County, Michigan* (Indianapolis, Ind., n.d.), 339–41.

ing, Stone adjusted machinery and output to meet the new demand, and by 1887 Flint salesmen were displaying fabric samples to custom-tailors and ready-to-wear manufacturers in Baltimore, New York City, and Rochester. Two years later, the mill also began the manufacture of men's wool pants for sale to consumers in the East and Middle West. Apparently profits received in the pants market failed to justify continuance of the line, so Stone launched an aggressive campaign to increase the volume of cloth sales to garment makers located closer to the factory. Consequently, by the turn of the century salesmen from Flint, supplied with samples, made regular calls on clothing manufacturers in Chicago, Cincinnati, Detroit, Indianapolis, and Milwaukee, in addition to visits to older, established customers in other cities.[12]

New owners assumed control of the mill in January 1900, but introduced few innovations except the disposal of all narrow looms, a step necessary to meet the demands of garment makers for fabrics in widths of at least fifty-four inches. The volume of sales to ready-to-wear manufacturers remained high, but after six months of operation the company failed to show a profit, and salesmen were immediately contacted and instructed to increase prices, thereby lowering the firm's ability to compete with eastern textile factories.[13] Flint's new managers were being educated in some of the techniques of selling to the clothing industry, and they soon learned that certain tactics used by garment manufacturers enhanced the instability of their market.

Garment makers placed cloth orders after examination of samples presented by mill agents or salesmen. In turn, manufacturers made up sample clothing to show to jobbers in the spring and fall. If jobbers disliked a particular line because of its pattern, style, or weave, garment makers often canceled the

12. See orders and correspondence in letter books of February 7, 1887–January 18, 1888; May 18, 1889–July 30, 1890; and December 22, 1899–May 27, 1900, in the Stone-Atwood Company Records, Michigan Historical Collections, University of Michigan, Ann Arbor.
13. Flint Woolen Mills to F. E. Larson, Flint, Michigan, July 5, 1900, Stone-Atwood Collection.

remainder of their order for that fabric, or returned remnants to textile mills claiming that they were either defective or unlike the sample.[14] Also, clothing manufacturers frequently placed their largest orders with big eastern factories, giving midwestern mills like Flint only the specialty orders for small pieces of cloth later in the season, expecting them to be rushed through the factory ahead of other fabrics already in process. Therefore, Flint's new owners initiated a general policy of allowing no cancelations, threatening to take the offending party to court if necessary in order to collect damages, and of refusing to accept small orders from manufacturers who were not regular customers. Despite these and other minor changes, Flint found it difficult to compete.

With only moderate success in selling to the ready-to-wear industry, Flint shifted production in 1904 to the manufacture of carriage cloth for sale to buggy factories in Indiana and Michigan, and within five years the plant had completely converted to that purpose. Large orders for carriage cloth allowed important economies of scale, but in their eagerness to specialize, and perhaps as a result of their previous experiences in the garment trades, Flint's managers instituted a new policy on the settlement of accounts which all but guaranteed the failure of the venture. Customers received no discounts for prompt payment of bills, and all carriage cloth was sold strictly on a "net" basis. "We allow no man a discount," an owner of the mill explained in response to an inquiry in 1909, furthermore, "we believe a manufacturer who will give discounts . . . is a coward."[15] Because they could usually expect to receive a 3 percent discount from other factories, buggymakers went elsewhere.

The new policy adopted on costing and prices added little to the prospects of success in the new line. After calculating net costs, and profits of 7 percent, Flint's managers added 1 percent to cover bad debts and incidental expenses. If raw wool prices

14. Ibid., February 6, 1900, Stone-Atwood Collection.
15. Flint Woolen Mills to the General Committee of Woolen and Worsted Manufacturers, Flint, Michigan, May 18, 1909, Stone-Atwood Collection.

increased or declined, the price of carriage cloth to buggy manufacturers received a corresponding adjustment.[16] By 1900, however, Michigan sheep no longer provided fleece in adequate quantities or of suitable quality. Therefore, Flint was compelled to dispatch a buyer to Montana and Wyoming each spring to obtain raw material. To figure their costs, buggymakers insisted on signing contracts for the future delivery of fabrics at set prices, but since the price of wool in the western market might fluctuate widely from year to year, Flint normally refused to make quotations on carriage cloth until all the raw product had been purchased in the Far West.[17] This impasse usually resulted in the loss of customers for the mill. In 1909, Flint yielded and signed a few set-price contracts, but lost money because of a miscalculation on the amount of wool that would be required to fill them.[18]

By the fall of 1909, Flint could no longer manufacture high-quality carriage cloth at a price competitive with textile factories located in the East. Suffering from a decline in business, several eastern woolen mills had turned to the production of carriage cloth during slack periods in an effort to keep machinery in operation and workers employed. "We are up against it pretty strong," wrote one of the Flint owners in October, because "they are willing to make carriage cloth for practically an exchange of dollars."[19] To resolve the problem, Flint's managers considered reentering the garment trade, even going so far as to contact a few of their old customers, but this idea never reached fruition.[20]

With Flint's machinery especially adapted to the manufac-

16. Ibid.

17. Flint Woolen Mills, Flint, Michigan, to Rex Buggy Company, June 27, 1908, Noyes Carriage Company, July 14, 1908, Mossman, Yarnelle and Company, May 27, 1909, and Henney Buggy Company, June 24, 1909, Stone-Atwood Collection.

18. Flint Woolen Mills to M. J. Smiley, Flint, Michigan, April 26, 1909, Stone-Atwood Collection.

19. Flint Woolen Mills to S. H. Curis, Flint, Michigan, October 11, 1909, Stone-Atwood Collection.

20. Flint Woolen Mills to Collings-Taylor Company, Flint, Michigan, October 13, 1909, Stone-Atwood Collection.

ture of one type of fabric, thoughts of regaining a foothold in the ready-to-wear trade displayed a certain lack of appreciation for the expenses and problems involved in such a move. Yet, the absence of perception regarding another sector of the market, geographically very close to the mill, demonstrated an even greater lack of foresight on the part of Flint's owners. Although they had noted the growth of the automobile industry in Michigan during the spring of 1909, the managers failed to perceive the future importance of the passenger car. In a letter to a friend in April, one of the owners seemed bewildered by the number of automobiles turned out every twenty-four hours, and further amazed at "where they go and how many people who buy automobiles and that cannot afford it."[21] From June through August 1909, the company passed up several requests for automotive top lining, preferring instead to stock carriage cloth for buggies.[22] Flint Woolen Mills closed in December of that year and the machinery was dismantled and sold. In September 1911 the city of Flint purchased the property for use as a community market.[23]

The early development of the Appleton Mills in Wisconsin resembled that of other midwestern woolen factories. W. W. Hutchinson, a native of Nova Scotia, moved from Canada to Appleton in 1858, procured a water-power site on the Fox River, and sometime during the early 1860s constructed a small woolen mill. This pioneer firm immediately offered custom-carding services to local farmers and within a few years supplied a host of rural merchants with coarse-quality cloth and yarn. Hutchinson had sold his controlling interest in the mill by 1881, the year a fire completely consumed the original building and all its machinery. A group of local investors, some of whom

21. Flint Woolen Mills to M. J. Smiley, Flint, Michigan, April 26, 1909, Stone-Atwood Collection.

22. "It looks very much as if we will have to let the automobile top lining pass this season as we will be obligated to make a liberal stock of carriage cloth during the summer months." Flint Woolen Mills to Mossman, Yarnelle and Company, Flint, Michigan, June 4, 1909, Stone-Atwood Collection.

23. *Textile World Record* 41 (September 1911): 734.

had migrated from New York to Wisconsin in the 1870s, incorporated a new company, ordered equipment, and in the spring of 1882 Appleton Mills resumed production.[24]

Apparently formulating a new strategy to increase sales in the Upper Midwest, Appleton's managers attempted to fill the void in the market created by the failure of other woolen mills in the region. This was the case in 1891, for example, when the factory hired an additional salesman to pick up the old customers of the Vassar Woolen Mills in southern Michigan. During the early 1890s three full-time salesmen traveled through the small towns of Michigan, Minnesota, and Wisconsin, showing cloth samples to local storekeepers.[25] In addition, Appleton also employed the Curtiss and Warren selling agency of Chicago to present their fabrics to ready-to-wear manufacturers in that city. Later in the decade, Appleton withdrew from the local market, released its salesmen, and sold exclusively through Elmer E. Rockwood, a dry goods commission merchant in Chicago who also marketed cloth in the East and Middle West for the Columbiaville Woolen Mills of Michigan. Rockwood called on clothiers and tailors, displayed fabrics, advised the mill on production, and solicited orders.[26]

Long before complete entrance into the garment trade, at least one manager at Appleton visualized the future importance of another midwestern business, which in time provided a growing market practically adjacent to the factory. Northern Wisconsin and Minnesota, and the Upper Michigan peninsula comprised one of the nation's leading papermaking regions, and Appleton's close proximity to firms in that industry offered distinct locational advantages to the company if subsidiary products needed by papermakers could be developed. For ap-

24. *Appleton* (Wis.) *Post-Crescent*, November 6, 1922; W. A. Goodspeed, *History of Outagamie County, Wisconsin* (Chicago, 1911), 1028; *History of Northern Wisconsin* (Chicago, 1881), 680.
25. Appleton Mills to Parker, Wilder and Company, Appleton, Wisconsin, April 18, 1891, in the Appleton Mills Collection, State Historical Society of Wisconsin, Madison.
26. For examples, see correspondence from Elmer E. Rockwood to Appleton Mills during February 1909 in the Appleton Collection.

proximately ten years, F. J. Harwood, the plant superintendent and a major stockholder, along with a handful of workers and department foremen, periodically conducted experiments on the fabrication of the endless, woven felts used on papermaking machines.[27] The manufacture of woolen felts required great technical skill, and although they had to meet exacting standards, no close substitutes existed for them. Therefore, Harwood realized that once Appleton could produce a high-quality felt the entire paper industry would open as a market. The mill invoiced its first felt in May 1890,[28] but for several more years Harwood and his associates worked closely with papermakers in the Fox River Valley, such as the Atlas Paper Company, a subsidiary of Kimberly-Clark, in an attempt to eliminate the numerous problems involved in their manufacture.[29] In July 1900, company salesmen reported that Appleton felts were finally established in the market and were capable of meeting all competitors, both in price and quality. Orders poured in. Appleton not only supplied paper mills in the Midwest, but quickly added felt customers located in Canada, the Middle Atlantic states, and New England.[30]

The flood of felt orders around 1900 seriously crowded the small plant and threatened to delay the production of fabrics for sale to the clothing industry. At a special meeting called in November 1902, the Appleton Board of Directors, acting on Harwood's recommendation, approved the acquisition of a woolen factory at Reedsburg, Wisconsin.[31] The Reedsburg

27. The technical requirements for the manufacture of papermakers' felts can be found in Dard Hunter, *Papermaking: A History and Technique of an Ancient Craft* (New York, 1947), 181, 565.

28. F. Harwood Orbison to Norman L. Crockett, Appleton, Wisconsin, June 29, 1967.

29. Appleton Mills, Appleton, Wisconsin, to W. S. Bartholew, May 11, 1891, and Kimberly-Clark, July 18, 1901, Appleton Collection.

30. For specific examples, see correspondence between F. J. Harwood and F. M. Towne during December 1900 and January 1901, in the Appleton Collection.

31. Minutes of the Board of Directors, Appleton Woolen Mills, November 13, 1902, in the possession of the company, Appleton, Wisconsin.

Woolen Mill had been constructed in 1881, incorporated in 1892, and by the time of the Appleton purchase contained four sets of cards and thirty-two broadlooms. Appleton transferred the manufacture of all piece goods to the newly acquired plant in Reedsburg, and converted the mill from water power to electricity in 1910. The company then contracted for an addition to the Appleton factory, ordering the necessary machinery to concentrate entirely on woven felts.[32]

In the sale of fabrics to the garment industry, fashion changes and order cancellations by no means constituted all the problems confronting Appleton Mills. In early 1909, Elmer Rockwood, the firm's representative in the East, impressed upon Harwood the necessity of altering the mill's production and marketing schedules. Rockwood argued that in the past Appleton had made up and shown too many samples too early in the season. Thus, by the time clothiers were ready to place orders with textile factories most had tired of Appleton designs. Wholesaling goods affected by fashion involved a high degree of risk, and few garment makers were willing to commit themselves to large cloth contracts far in advance of sales to their customers. The mill, therefore, would benefit by displaying a smaller variety of samples later in each season, allowing clothing manufacturers time to survey the market, and thereby enabling them to predict more accurately which combinations of fabrics and styles would produce the largest profits.[33]

Rockwood also counseled the mill on the need to consider another factor in the market which placed definite limits on manufacturing costs. For years, clothing retailers had clung to an irrational faith in rigid price brackets, and the influence of this unique phenomenon could be felt by all businesses serving the garment industry. If the price of a textile fabric exceeded some point, for example $1.00 per yard, most retailers assumed that there was no price short of the next bracket, perhaps $1.09

32. *Reedsburg* (Wis.) *Times Press*, February 25, 1954.
33. Elmer E. Rockwood to F. J. Harwood, Chicago, February 23, 1909, Appleton Collection.

per yard, for which it could be sold.[34] Since the entire industry seemed to share the belief in a discontinuous demand curve, mills were compelled to try to produce quality material at a reasonable profit, yet capable of competing in a particular price range. For the 1909 spring season, Rockwood advised Appleton to price its goods as close as possible to $1.00, $1.10, and $1.12½ to $1.15.[35]

At first, F. J. Harwood was undoubtedly shocked when his selling agent informed him that Appleton textiles were "too good." Rockwood went on to explain, however, that for the price, Appleton cloth represented the best buy in the trade, but other factories were offering lower grade, less-expensive goods which appeared to be of identical quality. Garment makers appreciated craftsmanship, but refused to pay an additional seven to ten cents per yard to obtain it because the average consumer of clothing proved incapable of distinguishing between subtle degrees of quality. Therefore, if the mill wished to remain in the market, manufacturing costs had to be reduced in order to bring Appleton prices more in line with those of competitors. As a second possibility, Rockwood recommended that the boss finisher be apprised of the situation and then urged to concentrate more of his efforts and skill on finishing cheaper material to enhance its surface appearance. "The fabrics that I want," wrote Rockwood in February 1909, "are the ones that look as good, even if they are not quite so good."[36]

Revenue received from the sale of papermakers' felts helped in part to sustain Appleton while the mill at Reedsburg sought an entree into the eastern clothing market. The demands of clothiers for postdated billing forced textile factories to carry customers for sixty to ninety days, sometimes longer, or to

34. Committee on Textile Price Research, Bureau of Economic Research, *Textile Markets: Their Structure in Relation to Price Research* (New York, 1939), 172. Since marginal mills cannot normally compete in these brackets, most are compelled to concentrate on "fancy" goods for special orders.
35. Elmer E. Rockwood to F. J. Harwood, Chicago, February 25, 1909, Appleton Collection.
36. Ibid.

liquidate the accounts receivable by selling them to a factor, who assumed the credit risk on such sales and advanced cash to cloth manufacturers. For these services, factors normally collected a fee amounting to 6 percent of the net sales.[37] In most industries factoring was considered a sign of weakness, but in woolen textiles it became an essential part of the financial operation of a small mill, and even the very largest concerns often found it to their interests to factor accounts. Felt profits failed to liberate Appleton from factoring, but they provided operating capital which carried the company through critical years, such as 1906 and 1908, when the Reedsburg operation lost money. Later, reinvestment of earnings in the plant at Reedsburg tended to keep it competitive.[38]

The policies adopted by the managers of Appleton, Faribault, Flint, and Watkins illustrated a few of the possibilities open to other mills in the Midwest during the last quarter of the nineteenth century. An overwhelming majority of the region's woolen factories ceased production after 1890, and in this respect Appleton and Faribault were unique. However, the problems faced by these two mills, Flint's inability to compete, and the Watkins's attempts to move farther west exemplified some of the frustrations experienced by other millowners. With Appleton as a possible exception, managers failed to formulate long-range strategies, instead reacting to alterations in the national market only when confronted with the unavoidable realization that past methods of operation were doomed to failure. And, of course, each delay in recognizing the obvious, and in planning for the future, sharply reduced the number of realistic alternatives open to the firm. Thus, the perception of managers at any given time relative to current

37. Prior to the 1890s, some commission houses and selling agents offered this service, but by the turn of the century a few banks had opened credit departments and started the purchase of "receivables." See Albert O. Greef, *The Commercial Paper House in the United States* (Cambridge, Mass., 1938), 104–105, and Owen T. Jones, "Factoring," *Harvard Business Review* 14 (Winter 1936): 186–99.

38. Corporate Minutes, Appleton Mills, in the possession of the company, Appleton, Wisconsin, and F. Harwood Orbison to Norman L. Crockett, Appleton, Wisconsin, September 9, 1965.

changes in the regional environment, and forecasts of how those variations might affect company prosperity, constituted an important factor in determining later success or failure. Lack of perception in anticipating change proved fatal in most cases.[39]

Flint's conversion from apparel fabrics to carriage cloth showed foresight. However, a lack of managerial ability and the failure to recognize how quickly the automobile would replace the horse and buggy quickly nullified most of the benefits arising from the transition. In retrospect, Flint's proximity to Detroit probably offered locational advantages equal to those of Appleton Mills and the western paper industry. It remains a mystery whether F. J. Harwood of Appleton developed the idea of producing endless, woven felts or if a Wisconsin papermaker first suggested it to him. Nevertheless, his determination to perfect their manufacture indicated he was convinced of their potentialities long before Appleton could successfully compete in the felt market. Harwood's diligence resulted in handsome profits and perhaps even the survival of the company. At Faribault, the shift from cloth to clothing and finally to blankets corresponded closely to the entrance of young blood into the firm during the 1890s and again in 1912. The need to experiment and innovate, recognized by the young managers at Faribault, along with the willingness of the older generation in the family dominated company to accept change, injected new life into the mill at important junctures in its development. Specialization on all-wool blankets, which began around 1900 and was nearly complete by 1914, placed the firm in a favorable position to seek and obtain government contracts from the army, but company records clearly indicate that Faribault was already well on the way to gaining a niche in the market for blankets before the advent of World War I. Conceivably, the Watkins brothers might have been attempting to realize some money

39. Of course, a few millowners in the Midwest may have anticipated the changes in the region's economy, but because of age, lack of capital, or the unwillingness to invest it, merely decided to continue production until profit margins no longer justified operation.

from the woolen mill by moving their old machinery west and selling it to a group of investors there. After reading the correspondence, however, it seems more plausible that the rural location of the factory and the brothers' deep involvement in farming and livestock-trading clouded their vision as to the realities of the situation. Namely, that the small, integrated woolen mill attempting to manufacture a complete line of coarse- and medium-quality cloth and serve a local market, symbolized a manufacturing unit of the past. Although some regions of the country still remained relatively isolated as late as 1900, the possibility of a profitable operation of these mills was vanishing.

The 113 small mills composing the midwestern woolen industry in 1909 shared a number of common problems, a few of which stemmed from their regional location. In an effort to discuss issues of mutual interest, representatives from eleven factories in the Midwest gathered in Chicago during July of that year, and the delegates organized the Western Woolen Manufacturers Association. Millowners from Indiana and Wisconsin dominated the original membership roster, which also listed executives from firms located in Michigan, Minnesota, and Missouri.[40] The new trade association almost immediately focused its attention on two major questions: the establishment of a uniform policy on the prepayment of freight which would place midwestern manufacturers on an equal basis with eastern textile mills, and an investigation of the prices charged by supply houses for frequently used dye goods.

Long before the Chicago meeting, midwestern woolen men

40. "Members of the Western Woolen Manufacturers Association," in the Appleton Collection. Contact and cooperation between the midwestern group and the National Association of Wool Manufacturers appears to have been negligible. Because of its dominance by carpet and worsted producers and its preoccupation with the tariff on imported wool, the NAWM no doubt offered little of interest to millowners in the Midwest. In 1871, for example, when the midwestern industry was near its peak, only a handful of wool manufacturers from the region were listed among the NAWM directors. See National Association of Wool Manufacturers, *Bulletin* 2 (October 1871): 553.

had complained that suppliers of soaps and dyes charged several different prices for the same item. To alleviate such discrimination and hoping to document their suspicions, WWMA members submitted old invoices of purchases from dye houses to a select committee for comparison and study.[41] The second problem proved more complex. Midwestern mills selling cloth in the Chicago market sought equality with eastern firms in regard to handling the payment of shipping costs. Chicago garment makers refused to pay the freight on fabrics shipped from midwestern factories until the account for such goods was settled. Since most accounts ran for at least sixty days, mills in the Midwest were burdened with the necessity of a cash outlay for the prepayment of transportation charges in addition to the normal extension of credit. On the other hand, eastern textile factories coerced clothing manufacturers in Chicago into paying all freight on delivery. Midwestern mills demanded the same privilege. Although several millowners seemed enthusiastic in the beginning, membership in the Western Woolen Manufacturers Association dwindled, meetings often lacked a quorum, and the organization apparently disbanded in 1914 before taking positive action on either problem.[42]

Beginning in 1873, the wholesale price index in the United States began a general downward trend lasting for approximately twenty-five years. All American manufacturers struggled with the decline, but the price of textiles, and especially woolen textiles, fell at a faster rate than most commodity groups. Moreover, increased competition from other fibers, such as cotton, and improved methods of reconstituting woolen rags into shoddy sharply reduced American per capita consumption of

41. F. J. Harwood to Davenport Woolen Mills, Appleton, Wisconsin, April 18, 1910, Appleton Collection.
42. F. J. Harwood to the Members of the Western Woolen Manufacturers Association, Appleton, Wisconsin, November 4, 1910, Appleton Collection. The minutes of the WWMA, in the Appleton Collection, gave no indication for the decline in interest among its members. By 1910, however, most mills in the Midwest had specialized, and it seems plausible that the number of problems common to all firms were not sufficient to encourage close cooperation.

127

wool after 1890.[43] Although the American woolen industry experienced few important combinations, over 350 woolen factories in New England and the Middle Atlantic states vanished from the census rolls between 1880 and 1900.[44] Thus, while manufacturers in the Midwest sought to compete with eastern textile mills, market pressures were eliminating less efficient firms throughout the country. The unhealthy state of the industry on the national level merely compounded the problems plaguing midwestern millowners and further helps to explain the nearly complete disappearance of these factories in one generation.

In 1870, the 881 woolen mills scattered throughout the eight states of the Middle West represented a combined capital investment of $14,604,372. However, these tiny factories constituted only 36 percent of all such establishments in the United States, and their capital investment comprised less than 10 percent of the industry total.[45] Despite their meager size, limited market, and the ephemeral nature of their existence, midwestern woolen mills accelerated the region's growth and development.

When measured in terms of capital investment, value of final output, and similar indexes, the woolen mills of the Midwest remained small in comparison to factories located along the Atlantic seaboard. To an eastern observer in the 1870s, production methods employed by a tiny midwestern firm would undoubtedly have seemed crude and inefficient. However, the character and size of the local market, along with the costs of

43. Norman S. B. Gras and Henrietta M. Larson, *Casebook in American Business History* (New York, 1939), 707; Chester W. Wright, *Wool-Growing and the Tariff* (Cambridge, Mass., 1910), 295–97.

44. U.S. Department of Commerce, Bureau of the Census, *Census of Manufactures: 1905, Textiles, Bulletin 74,* 130–36. Only one important combination existed in the industry. The American Woolen Company, organized in 1899, combined twenty-six woolen and worsted mills in the Northeast. In 1923 the corporation controlled fifty-nine factories in eight states. See Arthur Harrison Cole, "A Neglected Chapter in the History of Combinations: The American Wool Manufacture," *Quarterly Journal of Economics* 37 (May 1923): 439.

45. *Census of Manufactures: 1905, Textiles,* 130–36.

inputs and many other factors, determined economic efficiency. Manufacturing techniques utilized by a factory located in Massachusetts which sold fabrics in Boston might have resulted in failure if copied by a smaller mill in southern Iowa marketing finished cloth to farmers within fifty miles of the plant. Variations in transportation facilities, labor supplies, the depth of the market, and other considerations prompted millowners to apply a level of technology appropriate to a particular region or locality. The continued purchase and operation of obsolete machines in the Midwest long after the advent of improved equipment represented a case in point.

Directly, woolen mills and other types of residentiary manufacturing contributed little to the short-run economic development of the Middle West. Selling locally, and depending upon an abundant resource close to the factory, each firm merely floated on the prosperity of a small agricultural area. Since their marketing advantage rested almost entirely upon the ability to remain isolated from competitors, few manufacturers exhibited enthusiasm for the promotion of internal improvements which might encourage interregional trade. Moreover, the very nature of these enterprises prevented them from generating a significant number of backward or forward linkages leading to the formation and growth of subsidiary industries within the region. For example, rather than constructing plants in the Midwest, eastern textile machine builders sold new equipment through branch outlets in the region or consigned machinery to independent dealers there.

Indirectly, and over a period of time, regions derived benefits from the presence of a large number of these small residentiary factories. Perhaps their most important single contribution resulted from the simple production of goods for sale to people residing in relatively isolated areas. During the initial years of settlement the combination of high transportation costs and poor country roads excluded eastern manufactures from some portions of the midwestern market. The very existence of local factories and their ability to compete with finished commodities shipped into the region clearly indicated that goods manufactured in the Midwest were less expensive than those being imported from the outside. In addition, the custom services provided by most local concerns freed rural families from self-sufficiency, thereby allowing them to concentrate more of their labor on other pursuits, such as the production of staple crops.

Pioneer manufacturers also influenced the utilization and movement of capital and labor. Several eastern businessmen, possessing funds accumulated from other enterprises, were attracted to the Midwest by the possibilities of profitable investments in small woolen plants. To be sure, no single millowner commanded a large supply of capital, but the number of such people who were willing to migrate westward with their holdings constituted a substantial flow of funds into the region. More in the realm of speculation, it is possible that some of the money scraped together by manufacturers through small loans from family members and close friends would not have been employed in any other type of productive investment in the absence of these firms. This situation, observable in several developing nations, arises from the willingness of people to make sacrifices by foregoing current consumption in order to loan money to relatives.[46] As previously indicated, the low wages offered by most millowners in the Midwest prevented them from attracting skilled workers from the East. In 1870, however, the midwestern woolen industry provided at least part-time employment for approximately ten thousand people. And in many cases, jobs in pioneer mills supplemented rural incomes. For many persons toiling in midwestern factories these jobs were their first introduction to the routine of an organized industrial discipline. Thus, woolen mills and other types of residentiary manufacturing helped in part to break down the habits and mores of an agricultural society, and to prepare its citizens for more experienced participation in the full industrialization that soon occurred in the Midwest.

In their day, pioneer woolen mills served their surrounding territory well. Rural communities that were plagued with slow,

46. Eugene Staley, *Small Industry Development* (Menlo Park, Calif., 1958), 13.

costly, and unreliable transportation found the wool fabrics and yarn produced by such firms more to their liking than home-spun cloth. By accepting farm produce in exchange for custom services and fabrics, extending credit to merchants, and providing farmers with a convenient local market, such mills eased the scarcity of money in isolated areas. Sales methods and quests for capital speeded the growth of a mature credit and marketing system in the region. Yet, like other residentiary concerns, the tiny woolen mills of the Midwest fell victim to the very economic progress they had helped to create.

Bibliography

MANUSCRIPTS

Agawam Woolen Company Records. Merrimack Valley Textile Museum, North Andover, Massachusetts.

Appleton Mills Collection. The State Historical Society of Wisconsin, Madison, Wisconsin.

Brownell, Nathan Jr., Papers. Michigan Historical Collections, University of Michigan, Ann Arbor, Michigan.

C. G. Sargent Collection. Merrimack Valley Textile Museum, North Andover, Massachusetts.

Denney, Theodore, Letters. Indiana Historical Society, Indianapolis, Indiana.

Faulkner and Colony Collection. Manuscripts Division, Baker Library, Harvard University.

Island Woolen Mills Collection. The State Historical Society of Wisconsin, Madison, Wisconsin.

Johnson, Lothrop, Wool Purchase Book, 1859–1864. Michigan Historical Collections, University of Michigan, Ann Arbor, Michigan.

Lyman, Pliny S., Papers. Michigan Historical Collections, University of Michigan, Ann Arbor, Michigan.

Mauger and Avery Collection. Manuscripts Division, Baker Library, Harvard University.

McGraw, Thomas C., Papers. Burton Historical Collection, Detroit Public Library, Detroit, Michigan.

Murray, William, Woolen Mill Account Books. Indiana Historical Society, Indianapolis, Indiana.

North Star Woolen Mill Company Records. Minnesota Historical Society, St. Paul, Minnesota.

Northville Woolen Mills, Wool Books, 1864–1866. Michigan Historical Collections, University of Michigan, Ann Arbor, Michigan.

Stevens Collection. Merrimack Valley Textile Museum, North Andover, Massachusetts.

Stone-Atwood Company Records. Michigan Historical Collections, University of Michigan, Ann Arbor, Michigan.

Watkins Mill Collection. Jackson County, Missouri, Historical Society, Archives, Independence, Missouri.

Watkins Mill Papers. Private Collection of Mrs. Manfred Weber, Shawnee Mission, Kansas.

Watkins Mill Papers. Private Collection of Mrs. Ruth B. Roney, Lawson, Missouri.

BOOKS

American Sheep Producers Council. *Breeds of Sheep.* Denver, Colo., n.d.

Atherton, Lewis E. *Main Street on the Middle Border.* Bloomington, Ind., 1954.

——. *The Poineer Merchant in Mid-America.* University of Missouri Studies, 14, no. 2, (Columbia, Mo., 1939).

Bidwell, Percy W., and Falconer, John I. *History of Agriculture in the Northern United States, 1620–1860.* New York, 1941.

Biographical History of Genesse County, Michigan. Indianapolis, Ind., n.d.

Bridenbaugh, Carl. *The Colonial Craftsman.* New York, 1950.

Bryner, Edna. *The Garment Trades.* Cleveland, Ohio, 1916.

Budish, J. M., and Soule, George. *The New Unionism in the Clothing Industry.* New York, 1927.

Burnaby, Andrew. *Travels through the Middle Settlements in North America in the Years 1759 and 1760 with Observations upon the State of the Colonies.* Ithaca, N.Y., 1960.

Callender, Guy Stevens. *Selections from the Economic History of the United States, 1765–1860.* Boston, 1909.

Canfield, William H. *Outline Sketches of Sauk County.* Baraboo, Wis., 1872.

Carman, Ezra A., Heath, H. A., and Minto, John. *Special Report on the History and Present Condition of the Sheep Industry of the United States.* Washington, D.C., 1892.

Chandler, Alfred D., Jr. *Giant Enterprise: Ford, General Motors, and the Automobile Industry.* New York, 1964.

——. *Strategy and Structure: Chapters in the History of Industrial Enterprise.* Garden City, N.J., 1966.

Clark, Victor S. *History of Manufactures in the United States, 1607–1860.* Washington, D.C., 1916.

Clemen, Rudolf A. *The American Livestock and Meat Industry.* New York, 1923.

Cochran, Thomas C. *Basic History of American Business.* Princeton, N.J., 1959.

Cole, Arthur Harrison. *The American Wool Manufacture.* 2 vols. Cambridge, Mass., 1926.

Cole's Encyclopedia of Dry Goods. New York, 1900.

Committee on Textile Price Research, Bureau of Economic Research. *Textile Markets: Their Structure in Relation to Price Research.* New York, 1939.

Davis, Joseph S. *Essays in the Earlier History of American Corporations.* 2 vols. Cambridge, Mass., 1917.

Dooley, William H. *Textiles.* Boston, 1924.

DuPlessis, A. F. *The Marketing of Wool.* London, 1931.

Dyer, Elizabeth. *Textile Fabrics.* Boston, 1927.

Emmet, Boris, and Jeuck, John. *Catalogues and Counters: A History of Sears, Roebuck and Company.* Chicago, 1950.

Evans, Estwick. *A Predestrious Tour of Four Thousand Miles, through the Western States and Territories during the Winter of 1818.* Concord, Mass., 1819. In Reuben Gold Thwaites. *Early Western Travels.* 32 vols. Cleveland, Ohio, 1906, vol. 3.

Farmer, Silas. *The History of Detroit and Michigan.* Detroit, 1889.

Faulkner, Harold Underwood. *The Decline of Laissez Faire, 1897–1917.* New York, 1951.

Fite, Emerson D. *Social and Industrial Conditions in the North during the Civil War.* New York, 1910.

Forstman, Julius. *The Wool Manufacture in America and Europe.* Boston, 1911.

Garside, Alston Hill. *Wool and the Wool Trade.* New York, 1939.

Gibb, George S. *The Saco-Lowell Shops.* Cambridge, Mass., 1950.

Goodrich, Carter, and others. *Canals and American Economic Development.* New York, 1961.

Goodspeed, W. A. *History of Outagamie County, Wisconsin.* Chicago, 1911.

Gras, Norman S. B. *Industrial Evolution.* Cambridge, Mass., 1930.

——, and Larson, Henrietta M. *Casebook in American Business History.* New York, 1939.

Greef, Albert O. *The Commercial Paper House in the United States.* Cambridge, Mass., 1938.

Handlin, Oscar, and Handlin, Mary Flug. *Commonwealth: A Study of the Role of Government in the American Economy: Massachusetts, 1774–1861.* New York, 1947.

Historical Review of the State of Wisconsin: Its Industrial and Commercial Resources. New York, 1887.

History of Northern Wisconsin. Chicago, 1881.

Hollen, Norma, and Saddler, Jane. *Textiles.* New York, 1955.

Hunt, John W. *Wisconsin Gazetteer.* Madison, Wis., 1853.

Hunter, Dard. *Papermaking: A History and Technique of an Ancient Craft.* New York, 1947.

Jennings, Sister Marietta. *A Pioneer Merchant of St. Louis 1810–1820: The Business Career of Christian Wilt*. New York, 1939.

Jensen, Frederick G. *Capital Growth in Early America*. New York, 1965.

Jernegan, Marcus Wilson. *The American Colonies, 1492–1750*. New York, 1959.

Johnson, Emory R., and others. *History of Domestic and Foreign Commerce of the United States*. Washington, D.C., 1915.

Jones, Fred Mitchell. *Middlemen in the Domestic Trade of the United States*. Urbana, Ill., 1937.

Kirkland, Edward C. *Industry Comes of Age: Business, Labor, and Public Policy, 1860–1897*. New York, 1961.

Krug, Merton E. *History of Reedsburg and the Upper Baraboo Valley*. Madison, Wis., 1929.

Kuznets, Simon, and others. *Population Redistribution and Economic Growth, 1870–1950*. 3 vols. Philadelphia, 1960.

Magee, Mabel A. *Trends in Location of the Women's Clothing Industry*. Chicago, 1930.

Malott, Deane W., and Martin, Boyce F. *The Agricultural Industries*. New York, 1939.

Memorial and Genealogical Record of Dodge and Jefferson Counties, Wisconsin. Chicago, 1894.

Meyer, Duane. *The Heritage of Missouri—A History*. St. Louis, Mo., 1963.

Michl, Herman E. *The Textile Industries: An Economic Analysis*. Washington, D.C., 1938.

Missouri State Gazetteer and Business Directory, 1883–1884. St. Louis, Mo., 1884.

Morison, Samuel Eliot. *The Maritime History of Massachusetts, 1783–1860*. Boston, 1921.

Navin, Thomas R. *The Whitin Machine Works since 1831*. Cambridge, Mass., 1950.

Nettels, Curtis P. *The Emergence of a National Economy, 1775–1815*. New York, 1962.

Norris, James D. *Frontier Iron: The Maramec Iron Works 1826–1876*. Madison, Wis., 1964.

North, Douglass C. *The Economic Growth of the United States, 1790–1860*. Englewood Cliffs, N.J., 1961.

Nystrom, Paul H. *Economics of Fashion*. New York, 1928.

Perloff, Harvey S., and others. *Regions, Resources, and Economic Growth*. Baltimore, Md., 1960.

Pope, Jesse. *The Clothing Industry in New York*. University of Missouri Studies, 1, no. 1 (Columbia, Mo., 1905).

Proprietor of the Condensing Cards. *Statistics of the Woolen Manufactories in the United States*. New York, 1846.

Richards, Benjamin. *Textiles.* New York, 1939.

Richards, Florence S. *The Ready-to-Wear Industry, 1900–1950.* New York, 1951.

Schlesinger, Arthur M. *The Rise of the City, 1878–1898.* New York, 1933.

Shannon, Fred A. *The Organization and Administration of the Union Army, 1861–1865.* 2 vols. Cleveland, Ohio, 1928.

Sharkey, Robert P. *Money, Class, and Party: An Economic Study of Civil War and Reconstruction.* Baltimore, Md., 1959.

Shortfield, Luke. *The Western Merchant.* Philadelphia, 1849.

Staley, Eugene. *Small Industry Development.* Menlo Park, Calif., 1958.

Stevens, Horace. *Nathaniel Stevens, 1786–1865.* North Andover, Mass., 1946.

Stevens, Nathaniel. *Early Days of the Woolen Industry in North Andover, Massachusetts: A Sketch.* North Andover, Mass., 1925.

Strassmann, W. Paul. *Risk and Technological Innovation: American Manufacturing Methods during the Nineteenth Century.* Ithaca, N.Y., 1959.

Taussig, Frank W. *The Tariff History of the United States.* New York, 1923.

Taylor, George Rogers, and Neu, Irene D. *The American Railroad Network, 1861–1890.* Cambridge, Mass., 1956.

Textile Manufacturers' Directory. New York, 1883.

The History of Linn County, Missouri. Kansas City, Mo., 1882.

Tryon, Rolla M. *Household Manufactures in the United States, 1640–1860.* Chicago, 1917.

Ware, Norman. *The Industrial Worker, 1840–1860.* Gloucester, Mass., 1959.

Welby, Adlard. *A Visit to North America and the English Settlements in Illinois.* London, 1821. In Reuben Gold Thwaites. *Early Western Travels.* 32 vols. Cleveland, Ohio, 1906, vol. 12.

Wentworth, Edward Norris. *America's Sheep Trails, History, Personalities.* Ames, Iowa, 1948.

Wiley, Bell I. *The Life of Billy Yank.* New York, 1952.

Wright, Chester W. *Wool-Growing and the Tariff.* Cambridge, Mass., 1910.

ARTICLES

Atherton, Lewis E. "Auctions as a Threat to American Business in the Eighteen Twenties and Thirties," *Bulletin of the Business Historical Society* 11 (November 1937): 104–107.

———. "Early Western Mercantile Advertising," *Bulletin of the Business Historical Society* 12 (September 1938): 52–57.

———. "James and Robert Aull—A Frontier Missouri Mercantile Firm," *Missouri Historical Review* 30 (October 1935): 3–27.

Baxter, Maurice D. "Encouragement of Immigration to the Middle West during the Era of the Civil War," *Indiana Magazine of History* 46 (March 1950): 25–38.

Beale, Howard K. "The Tariff and Reconstruction," *American Historical Review* 35 (January 1930): 276–94.

Blegen, Theodore C. "The Competition of the Northwestern States for Immigrants," *Wisconsin Magazine of History* 3 (September 1919): 3–29.

Brown, Harry James. "The Fleece and the Loom: Wool Growers and Wool Manufacturers during the Civil War," *Business History Review* 29 (March 1955): 1–27.

Callender, Guy Stevens. "The Early Transportation and Banking Enterprises of the States in Relation to the Growth of Corporations," *Quarterly Journal of Economics* 18 (November 1902): 111–62.

Carter, Harvey L. "Rural Indiana in Transition, 1850–1860," *Agricultural History* 20 (April 1946): 107–21.

Cherington, Paul T. "Some Aspects of the Wool Trade of the United States," *Quarterly Journal of Economics* 25 (February 1911): 337–56.

Coben, Stanley. "Northeastern Business and Radical Reconstruction," *Mississippi Valley Historical Review* 46 (June 1959): 67–90.

Clark, Victor S. "Manufacturing Development during the Civil War," in Ralph Andreano, ed., *The Economic Impact of the American Civil War.* Cambridge, Mass., 1962, 41–48.

Cole, Arthur Harrison. "A Neglected Chapter in the History of Combinations: The American Wool Manufacture," *Quarterly Journal of Economics* 37 (May 1923): 436–75.

———. "Agricultural Crazes," *American Economic Review* 16 (December 1926): 622–39.

Connor, L. G. "A Brief History of the Sheep Industry in the United States," American Historical Association, *Report* 1 (1918): 89–197.

Crockett, Norman L. "A Study of Confusion: Missouri's Immigration Program, 1865–1916," *Missouri Historical Review* 62 (April 1963): 248–60.

———. "The Westward Movement and the Transit of American Machine Technology: The Case of Wool Manufacturing," *Nebraska Journal of Economics and Business* 8 (Summer 1969): 111–20.

Davis, Lance E. "Capital Immobilities and Finance Capitalism: A Study of Economic Evolution in the United States, 1820–1890," *Explorations in Entrepreneurial History,* vol. 1, 2d ser. (Fall 1963): 88–105.

Due, John F. "The Rise and Decline of the Midwest Interurban," *Current Economic Comment* 14 (August 1952): 36–51.

Fenstermaker, J. Van. "A Description of Sangamon County, Illinois, in 1830," *Agricultural History* 39 (July 1965): 136–40.

Freudenberger, Herman, and Redlich, Fritz. "The Industrial Development of Europe: Reality, Symbols, Images," *Kyklos* no. 3, 17 (1964): 272–403.

Gibson, George H. "The Growth of the Woolen Industry in Nineteenth Century Delaware," *Textile History Review* 5 (October 1964): 125–57.

Glazer, Sidney. "The Rural Community in the Urban Age: The Changes in Michigan since 1900," *Agricultural History* 23 (April 1949): 130–34.

Hanna, Mary Alice. "The Trade of the Delaware District before the Revolution," *Smith College Studies in History* 2 (1917): 239–343.

Heaton, Herbert. "Benjamin Gott and the Anglo-American Cloth Trade," *Journal of Economic and Business History* 2 (November 1929): 146–62.

"Investing in Modern Management: The 'free form' Corporation," Equity Research Associates, *Bulletin*, September 20, 1966.

Jones, Owen T. "Factoring," *Harvard Business Review* 14 (Winter 1936): 186–99.

Kemmerer, Donald L. "Financing Illinois Industry, 1830–1890," *Bulletin of the Business Historical Society* 27 (June 1953): 97–111.

"Large Midwestern Woolen Mill Founded by German Cabinetmaker," *America's Textile Reporter* 75 (June 8, 1961): 47–49, 58.

Maclaurin, W. R., and Meyers, Charles A. "Wages and the Movement of Factory Labor," *Quarterly Journal of Economics* 57 (February 1943): 241–64.

Marburg, Theodore F. "Manufacturers Drummer, 1852, with Comments on Western and Southern Markets," *Bulletin of the Business Historical Society* 22 (April 1948): 106–14.

Martin, Margaret E. "Merchants and Trade of the Connecticut River Valley, 1750–1820," *Smith College Studies in History* 24 (1938): 1–284.

Pursell, Carroll W., Jr. "E. I. Dupont and the Merino Mania in Delaware, 1805–1815," *Agricultural History* 26 (April 1962): 91–100.

———. "E. I. Dupont, Don Pedro, and the Introduction of Merino Sheep into the United States, 1801: A Document," *Agricultural History* 33 (April 1959): 86–88.

———. "Thomas Digges and William Pearce: An Example of the Transit of Technology," *William and Mary Quarterly* 21 (October 1964): 551–60.

Robinson, Dwight E. "Fashion Theory and Product Design," *Harvard Business Review* 36 (November–December 1958): 126–38.

―――. "The Importance of Fashion in Taste to Business History: An Introductory Essay," *Business History Review* 37 (Spring–Summer 1963): 5–36.

Schmidt, Louis Bernard. "Internal Commerce and the Development of a National Economy before 1860," *Journal of Political Economy* 47 (December 1939): 798–822.

Shannon, Fred A. "A Post Mortem on the Labor-Safety-Valve Theory," *Agricultural History* 19 (January 1945): 31–37.

Siegthaler, Hansjorg. "What Price Style? The Fabric-Advisory Function of the Drygoods Commission Merchant, 1850–1880," *Business History Review* 41 (Spring 1967): 36–61.

Smolensky, Eugene, and Ratajcak, Donald. "The Conception of Cities," *Explorations in Entrepreneurial History*, vol. 2, 2d ser. (Winter 1965): 90–131.

Stewart, Peter. "A Brief History of the Peace Dale Manufacturing Company, 1802–1918," *Textile History Review* 4 (January 1963): 12–23.

―――. "A Profit-Sharing System for the Peace Dale Mill in Rhode Island," *Textile History Review* 4 (July 1963): 126–33.

Sullivan, William A. "The Industrial Revolution and the Factory Operative in Pennsylvania," *Pennsylvania Magazine of History and Biography* 78 (October 1954): 476–94.

Taeuber, Conrad. "Rural-Urban Migration," *Agricultural History* 15 (July 1941): 151–60.

Tiebout, Charles M. "Location Theory, Empirical Evidence, and Economic Evolution," Regional Science Association, *Papers and Proceedings* 3 (1957): 74–86.

Tonning, Wayland A. "Department Stores in Down State Illinois, 1889–1943," *Business History Review* 29 (December 1955): 335–49.

―――. "The Beginnings of the Money-Back Guarantee and the One Price Policy in Champaign-Urbana, Illinois, 1833–1880," *Business History Review* 30 (June 1956): 196–210.

Viles, Jonas. "Old Franklin: A Frontier Town of the Twenties," *Mississippi Valley Historical Review* 9 (March 1923): 269–82.

"War as a Stimulus to American Industry," *Bulletin of the Business Historical Society* 8 (January 1934): 49–52.

Weld, L. D. H. "Specialization in the Woolen and Worsted Industry," *Quarterly Journal of Economics* 27 (November 1912): 67–94.

Wilson, Harold F. "The Rise and Decline of the Sheep Industry in Northern New England," *Agricultural History* 9 (January 1935): 12–40.

Woodman, Harold F. "Itinerant Cotton Merchants of the Antebellum South," *Agricultural History* 40 (April 1966): 79–90.

GOVERNMENT DOCUMENTS AND PUBLIC RECORDS

Andrews, Israel D. *Trade and Commerce of the British North American Colonies, and upon the Great Lakes and Rivers, 1854,* 32d Cong., 1st sess., Senate Exec. Doc. 112.

Dominion of Canada, Department of Agriculture. *The Sheep Industry in Canada, Great Britain, and United States.* Ottawa, 1911.

Fifteenth Annual Report of the Commissioner of Labor, 1900: A Compilation of Wages in Commercial Countries from Official Sources. Washington, D.C., 1900.

Jesness, O. B., and Kerr, W. H. *Cooperative Purchasing and Marketing Organizations among Farmers in the United States,* USDA, Bulletin 547.

Missouri State Board of Agriculture. *Report, 1868.*

Newcomb, H. T. *Changes in the Rate of Charge for Railroads and Other Transportation Services,* USDA, Div. of Stat., Misc. ser. Bulletin 15.

Ninth Biennial Report of the Bureau of Labor of the State of Minnesota, 1903–1904. Minneapolis, Minn., 1904.

Report of the Commissioner of Agriculture, 1862, 37th Cong., 3d sess., House Exec. Doc. 78.

Report of the Commissioner of Patents, Agriculture, 1845, 29th Cong., 1st sess., House Doc. 140.

Report of the Commissioner of Patents for the Year 1851, 33d Cong., 1st sess., House Exec. Doc. 39.

The Wool Trade of the United States, 61st Cong., 1st sess., Senate Misc. Doc. 70.

U.S. Department of Labor, Bureau of Statistics. *Bulletin 128* (1913), *Bulletin 150* (1914), *Bulletin 238* (1915).

U.S. Bureau of Statistics. *Wool and Manufactures of Wool.* Washington, D.C., 1888.

U.S. Department of Commerce, Bureau of the Census. *Census of Manufactures: 1905, Textiles, Bulletin 74.*

——. *Eleventh Census, Agriculture: 1890.*

——. *Fourteenth Census, Manufacturing, 1919.*

——. *Ninth Census, The Statistics of the Population of the United States, 1870.*

——. *Abstract of the Twelfth Census, 1900.*

——. *Thirteenth Census, Agriculture.*

U.S. Department of Commerce, Census Office. *Manufactures of the United States in 1860: Compiled from the Original Returns of the Eighth Census.*

U.S. Department of Commerce, Fourth Census, 1820. *Manufactures, State of Indiana.* Microfilm in the Indiana State Library, Archives Division, Indianapolis, Indiana.

U.S. Tariff Board. *Wool and Manufactures of Wool.* Washington, D.C., 1912.

Wholesale Prices, Wages, and Transportation, 52nd Cong., 2d sess., Senate Report 1394.

NEWSPAPERS AND PERIODICALS

Appleton (Wis.) *Post-Crescent,* November 6, 1922.

Armour's Livestock Bureau, *Monthly Letter to Animal Husbandmen,* 13.

Commercial and Financial Chronicle, New York, 7.

Fibre and Fabric, Boston, 13, 21, 53, 68.

Franklin, Missouri *Intelligencer,* April 22, 1823.

Hunt's Merchants' Magazine and Commercial Review, New York, 24.

Indianapolis Star, August 9, 1942.

Indianapolis Sunday Star, August 27, 1911, October 26, 1930.

Jackson, (Mo.) *Independent Patriot,* May 26, 1821.

Liberty (Mo.) *Tribune,* May 10, 1861, April 16, 24, 1863, June 24, 1864.

Liberty (Mo.) *Weekly Tribune,* April 27, June 8, 1860.

Minneapolis Daily Tribune, August 15, 1875.

National Association of Wool Manufacturers, *Bulletin,* 2, 38.

Niles' National Register, Baltimore, Md., 72.

Reedsburg (Wis.) *Times Press,* February 25, 1954.

Textile World, New York, 18, 19, 20, 21, 23, 24.

Textile World Record, Boston, 25, 41.

The Lexington (Mo.) *Intelligencer,* October 6, 1877.

The Western Journal of Agriculture, Manufactures, Mechanic Arts, Internal Improvement, Commerce, and General Literature, St. Louis, 2.

The Woolen Mill News, Louisville, August 1, 1875.

Woolen Manufacturers' Association of the Northwest, *First Annual Report,* 1868.

UNPUBLISHED WORKS

Brown, Harry James. "The National Association of Wool Manufacturers, 1864–1897." Ph.D. diss., Cornell University, 1948.

Copy of "An Interview, Lucile Kane with William G. Northup, in the Minneapolis Offices of the North Star Woolen Mills," November 16, 1949. Minnesota Historical Society, St. Paul.

Crawford, Finla G. "The Wool Industry of the United States, 1865–1870." M.A. thesis, University of Wisconsin, 1916.

Klemer, Frank H. "The History of the Faribault Woolen Mills." Paper read before the Rice County, Minnesota, Historical Society, October 22, 1940. Minnesota Historical Society, St. Paul.

Studley, Robert L. "The Marketing and Financing of Wool." Address delivered before the Robert Morris Associates, Boston, November 17, 1923. Baker Library, Harvard University.

Index

Design by James Wageman

Composed & printed in Linotype Primer
Kingsport Press